FINDING THE LUMINOUS FIELD

~ SHANTI HUEBNER ~

FINDING THE LUMINOUS FIELD

Mana Retreat Centre
608 Manaia Road, RD1
Coromandel, 3581, New Zealand

Available from Mana Retreat Centre, Amazon.com and other retail outlets, and on Kindle and other devices.

DISCLAIMER: This book includes an anthology of works collected for educational purposes, and contains the opinions and ideas of its author and the many other sources reviewed. It is intended to provide useful and informative material on the subject matter covered, with the understanding that the author is not engaged in rendering counseling or any other kind of personal professional services in this publication.

Any mention of trademarks or trademarked names is for informational purposes only. The author's use of any copyrighted material or trademark does not imply approval, sponsorship, association or endorsement by the owners of these trademarks or copyrights. Furthermore, the mention of products or services does not imply endorsement by the author or publisher.

This book is not for profit. Proceeds will be donated to the Mana Charitable Trust.

FULL COLOUR EDITION

ISBN-13: 978-1537578224
ISBN-10: 1537578227

DEDICATED TO the exploration and awakening of consciousness and to my beloved husband Rainer in gratitude for this precious gift of love, a refuge for my tender, wild heart and a "wind beneath my wings".[1]
In love... always in love.

ACKNOWLEDGMENTS

It is with much joy that I offer this book to you. Woven into it you will find inspirational sayings, poems and teaching stories that have been a light on my path. May you find insights to reflect on, teachings to ponder, stories that touch you and most of all a warm feeling as you and I connect through these pages. My heart reaches out to yours as we touch that luminous field together.

Where possible, the sources for statements of fact and quotations are identified in the text. Other background sources include the following.

I would like to deeply acknowledge and honour my first teacher, Swami Shyam of the International Meditation Institute in Kullu, India and recipient of the Yog Shiromani award from the President of India. His book *Light of Knowledge* and many others transformed my way of looking at life. More than anything though, his teachings *(satsangs,* in Sanskrit[2]), are what stay with me, and I offer some of his wisdom taken from my notes over many years and from my memory.

From the Sufi path I have received so much inspiration, including poems from Hafiz (Shams-ud-din Muhammad Hafiz of Shirazi, 1320-1389) (i.e. in *The Gift* translated by Daniel Ladinsky) and the poems of Rumi (Jalāl ad-Dīn Muhammad Rūmī, 1207-1273) found in various collections of his work such as *Like This* translated by Coleman Barks and *Love Poems from God* translated by Daniel

Ladinsky. Collections of the works of Hazrat Inayat Khan (1882-1927) have been an inspiration, including *The Sufi Message of Hazrat Inayat Khan*, *The Unity of Religious Ideals* and *The Inner Life*. Thank you Murshid Samuel Lewis for the Dances of Universal Peace. I would also like to thank Atum and Halima McEwan, Sufi mentors and guides.

I spent much time studying the ancient Goddess traditions. Many books helped me with this journey but I will mention *When God Was a Woman* by Merlin Stone and *Goddesses in Every Woman* by Jean Bolen. I thank Carmen Boulter for initiating me into the mysteries of ancient Egypt, and all of the many women I have shared circles with over the years – we really dug deep together.

In exploring the shamanic cultures and being with indigenous people, I was especially affected by the time I spent with them in ritual and sacred spaces such as sweat lodges. I would like to thank you for sharing your energy, insights and wisdom.

After a near death experience when I encountered very powerfully the energy of Christ, the mystical message of Jesus touched me deeply. Joel Goldsmith's books, *The Infinite Way* and *The Realisation of Oneness* have been constant reminders to me through the years. References to the Bible (and to Jesus' teachings) are to the King James Version of the Holy Bible, unless otherwise indicated.

I bow to Lama Yeshe and Lama Zopa who introduced me to Tibetan Buddhism. The Dalai Lama has been an inspiration to me, and I thank Prema and Anahata for the auspicious opportunity to dance the 21 praises of Tara for him in Dharamsala. I also leaned into the wisdom of the ancients, including the *Buddhavacana* (religious texts accepted as the words of the Buddha) and the *Vedas* (early Hindu religious texts).

Many other contemporary teachers have influenced me deeply through courses taken, discourses attended, and retreats with them. These include Gangaji (www.gangaji.org) as well as Adyashanti, a Zen teacher/author (www.adyashanti.org); Tarchin Hearn (*Daily Puja*, greendharmatreasury.org); Eckhart Tolle, whose books include

Stillness Speaks, *The Power of Now* and *A New Earth: Awakening to Your Life's Purpose*; and Zen Master Thích Nhat Hanh, global spiritual leader, poet and peace activist, now of Plum Village, France and the author of over 100 books including *Being Peace* and *The Long Road Turns to Joy* (www.plumvillage.org) as well as *Vispassana* meditation retreats with gifted teachers like Joseph Goldstein. My time in Taizé has been rich with insights and music and I am also so very grateful to my sound teacher Ruth Weimer and her mentor Frau Gisela Rohmert for sharing their knowledge and guidance, and to Tony Backhouse for his gift of song.

To my mother – her love and her caring are with me every day and I give thanks for all that she taught me and her incredible kindness. To my sister Penny whose love, encouragement and tireless editing have been a wonderful support. She has been amazing. To my brothers: Bob who kick-started me on my path and Dave whose courage has been such an inspiration; and to all my family, especially my four children: Karina, Kyla, Tanya and Sasha and their partners and children – I love you all dearly. Thank you for being in my life. All my dear friends, our Mana/Dharma Gaia community, my dance family, Tara choir (my singing *sangha*) – you are all my teachers. Also a big thanks to my pre-readers Jane and Penelope. And finally, I am so grateful to my life partner Rainer. We share so much and he is such an incredible support and companion.

Thank you all from my heart.

TABLE OF CONTENTS

Today may there be peace within.
May you trust that you are exactly where you are meant
to be.
May you not forget the infinite possibilities that are
born of faith in yourself and others.
May you use the gifts that you have received and pass
on the love that has been given to you.
May you be content with yourself just the way you are.
Let this knowledge settle into your bones, and allow
your soul the freedom to sing, dance, praise and love.
It is there for each and every one of us.

~ St. Thérèse of Lisieux (1873-1897)

INTRODUCTION

This book is in part a memoir of a spiritual journey, written as a way to share teachings that have touched me and lit my path as well as insights that have expanded my capacity to experience peace and to find my way home to love. May they also be a light on your path.

Life is a journey of discovery and an extraordinary opportunity to awaken. Various traditions offer different spiritual paths and choose their own labels for what they venerate, including the One, God, the All, the Source, the Great Spirit, Life, Love, Existence, or pure consciousness, to name a few. After a lifetime of studying and embracing many of these traditions, I believe that there is no right or wrong label or path, and that for those who seek, the ultimate destination is the same. Your label may not be mine, but I expect one day we will all meet in that "luminous field".

Our journey together begins with a chapter describing the spiritual paths I have travelled over my 65 years. Each contributed to my growth; perhaps you will find something that strikes a chord with you. In the second chapter you'll read about the blessings, tragedies and experiences that led me to the "still point", and its nature. In the next chapter, after exploring interbeing, we'll look at the dance of relationships. I'll share some of what I've gleaned while taking and teaching innumerable courses (and from life) about love, marriage, reconnecting after a falling out, and if all else fails, the secret to an amiable separation. The fourth chapter is a useful condensation of Buddhist principles that you'll refer to often if you have an affinity with that path. This is followed by a paper I wrote during my graduate studies in metaphysics, "The Healing Power of Sound" – a topic dear to me. Then I apply what I have learned in a series of letters and other writings on dealing with regret and stress, generosity, love, finding yourself and happiness in chapter six. Finally, I include essays and poems written at transformational moments in my life – "Coming Home (Stories from my Life Learnings)". In the Resources you will find my personal keys to well-being, worksheets, tools and other material for inquiry I hope will be of interest. I invite you to take your time, and allow yourself the space for reflection and contemplation as you read.

Time flies when you're in the body; or as Adyashanti says, "Time flies when there isn't any".[3] Sometimes you just know when it's time: the fruit is ripe, ready to fall – you don't have to pull it off the tree, it just drops. About fifteen years ago a friend of my mother's said to me, "You need to write a book", but it wasn't time. Now the fruit is ripe. It's the autumn of my life and it's simply time.

CHAPTER ONE: THE JOURNEY WITHIN

The journey is the goal.[4]

My life has been very blessed, in part I believe because trauma and tragedy struck early and hard. That suffering inspired a lifelong journey to find and know the truth.

Life has offered me opportunities to travel widely and study deeply in my search for meaning, fulfillment and freedom. My journey has led me to every continent and along many paths. In my twenties the search meant spending what little I had on airfares to live in countries like Spain and India, bringing not much more than my child, a musical instrument and whatever clothing would fit in my backpack along with the tools of my jewellery-making trade. Life led me to New Zealand in 1974 and later to co-founding and creating Mana Retreat Centre, where we have been able to invite cutting edge teachers. From there I continued travelling to some of the great spiritual centres of our time. Eventually I came to see (and try to live) what to me seem to be universal truths. It's time to share what I've learned with you, and I trust you will do the same for me.

Five decades into my journey, the core questions have been these. Who am I? What does it mean to awaken and to live consciously, and how does one go about exploring and living that?

What about conscious dying; how can we prepare for our exit from this realm? And finally, what is spiritual community and how can it support this process? How can we create pockets of people worldwide working together towards awakening for the sake of all beings?

My Personal Journey

My spiritual quest started in earnest in Canada after I gave up my first child, Karina, for adoption in April 1970. I was very young, frightened and confused. Two weeks after this devastating loss I was trying desperately to get her back, but to no avail. I entered a dark night of the soul that would really be the beginning of my journey, and this took me to inner depths I had not known before. After a period of darkness and depression, the extraverted energy of youth was turned inwards on a search for truth, for freedom, and though I didn't realise it at the time, for awakening. I needed to find out the truth of who I was and what I was here for, as well as my relationship to whatever higher power might exist.

I had always felt Spirit to be guiding my life, but at this stage in my late teens, that still felt like something separate and outside of me. When I started transcendental meditation in 1973 on the advice of my brother Bob, diligently doing my morning and evening 20 minute sits, a whole new inner world opened for me and my meditation became a place of refuge. That same year I began a practice of tai chi with Master Mok, a wonderful Chinese master in Edmonton, Canada. This served to ground me more and more into the present moment. These mindful movements of tai chi brought me much peace and inner tranquillity. I also began a yoga practice that same year. This is a practice that to this day sustains me and supports that inner state of union that yoga is all about. Yoga has been a real touchstone all these years, bringing me home to my true self, and has really helped to keep my body supple and my energy flowing. (I share my personal keys to well-being in Resource 1.)

Later that same year (1973) my daughter Kyla was born. Her presence in my life was, and still is, an absolute delight. When she was only ten days old, her father Sol and I moved to Valle Gran Rey – the Valley of the Great King – on La Gomera, one of the least known of the Canary Islands. Here, white-washed villas spill down the side of the mountain towards black sand beaches punctuated by date palms. We lived with our newborn near the top of the mountain surrounded by ancient water ducts and terraces. Our Spanish neighbours simply adored our little red-headed girl. We spent this precious time getting to know this beautiful soul and doing our practices of tai chi, meditation and yoga. However, after a scary encounter with hepatitis, with my partner getting terribly ill, we returned to Canada in 1974 when Kyla was six months old.

We arrived just in time for a synchronistic meeting with my first real spiritual master – an Indian guru (which simply means teacher) called Swami Shyam. Something shifted in me that day which began the inner journey of awakening that I knew to be a major purpose of my life – to come home to who I really am, to learn to know myself as a being of light and love, and to begin the process of releasing the many beliefs and habit patterns which were obscuring that light. I was ready and willing to leap into this unknown realm; it was calling me louder than anything ever had before. (In a while, I'll share more about this time with Swami-Ji.)

Three years later, in 1977, I would journey to India with my wee family to spend more in-depth time around this enlightened master. But meanwhile I had plenty of work to do, exploring the layers of identification which were making themselves known to me. This process of awakening is often compared to the peeling of an onion where you continue until eventually there is nothing left, just space. We find that all these layers we are identified with (the body, the emotions, the mind) are just our vehicles, not the whole truth of who we really are. The truth is free from birth and death, free from all that we thought was "me".

Over those years after I lost Karina to adoption, I found it very helpful to work with my suffering and grief in encounter groups and various therapies. These enabled me to release the intense pain I was experiencing, as well as to discover where I was still caught up and holding on; old patterns that I still clung tightly to. In 1976 when my brother Bob took his life (I talk more in depth about this later), this was another massive loss and a time of intense transformation for me. Bob was my friend and spiritual companion as well as my brother. Although he had been such a nuisance when we were younger, all that changed in our late teens. His passing catapulted me to another level of grief and deep longing to not only free myself for my own sake, but for his and for the many others suffering in this arena we call life. The *bodhisattva* was awakening in me – a call to wake up for the sake of all beings.

It was a couple of weeks after Bob's passing that I did my first *Vipassana,* a ten day retreat in total silence with many hours a day of meditation. With death and loss totally present for me this was very powerful. There were moments of dissolving and even disintegrating. One evening, after a long meditation, I was sitting outside in a swathe of moonlight, my body in touch with the earth and my mind empty, at peace. Someone drifted past and their shawl touched my shoulder, but my experience of this was that the molecules of the shawl and my shoulder actually passed through each other. We were interbeing. It was very healing and I felt my brother's presence with me and his love. I was touching levels of the formless that they speak about in Buddhism, experiencing a liberating sense of emptiness.

It was so agonising and heart-wrenching to feel my parents' grief around my brother's passing on top of my own. He was only 23 and my mom's baby. She carried that ache in her heart but tried so bravely to get on with life. Just writing this brings tears of deep compassion to my eyes as I am now a mother of four and a grandmother of six, and I can only imagine her suffering. She had lost her first husband Jack Love in the war, her closest sister Honey in the 1960's and not many years later she lost her second husband in a tragic accident (see Chapter 2). She was one courageous soul.

Transformation was happening thick and fast for me around the time of my brother's death. Thankfully I was beginning to gather the tools in my medicine bag to enable me to be present for what life was offering. I began to see how important it is to just be with what is rather than resist it. That doesn't mean it will be easy, but so often it is our resistance to life, to what is, that causes the major part of our suffering.

Not long after Bob's passing (about three months later in 1976), we came back to New Zealand from Canada, and were part of the early days of a community on the Coromandel Peninsula called Karuna Falls. Here we were pioneering, building and planting gardens, and living close to the earth. I shared a little hut with my daughter Kyla down by the river and did my washing in the rushing stream. We ate outside under the stars and experienced those back to the land "hippy" years of the mid 70's. Kyla was such a joy to be with and we did everything together. It was fun, hard work, challenging and an incredible experience. During this time I met and studied with a number of Buddhist teachers, such as Lama Yeshe and Lama Zopa, and took various initiations from them. I met and was taught by Indian yogis, and learned more about herbal remedies and growing food organically. And it was while I was living at Karuna and holding small meditation/chanting gatherings that I met Rainer, who was to be my beloved life partner (but I didn't know that yet!).

In 1977 we finally made it to India and I came to understand why people say that you either love India or hate it, as it is a land of extremes – from parched desert to steaming jungle, tin huts to the Taj Mahal, no-tech to high tech. I loved it. I felt like I had found a home for my wandering soul at the ashram in Kullu – Valley of the Gods – where I was to study with Swami-Ji. Later, I also spent a few months in Poona with a teacher then called Bhagwan Shree Rajneesh.

That was a wild time of dance and encounter groups, learning my first Dances of Universal Peace, at the time called Sufi dances.

On the way back to Kullu in early 1978, our train clattered north carrying us from the smog and teeming streets of New Delhi towards another world: the pine-scented air of the Himalayan foothills. Clambering down from one last local bus at journey's end, I remember pausing to admire snow-crowned peaks highlighted against a rose and gold sky, and turning to climb the familiar hundred plus steps to a warm welcome at the ashram. I felt that there I had found my heart teacher.

To this day I give deep thanks for the guidance Swami-Ji gave me in directing me to my inner self. This seemed to begin to quench the thirst that I had not yet been able to satisfy. Here I received clear direction, and living in the ashram was an incredibly valuable experience for me. Many hours were spent in meditation and finding that inner place of tranquility where I could feel such a joy, such a peace. He was always guiding me within. Yet one had to stay alert for the unexpected. One evening during an all night meditation, I sleepily got up to go outside to the loo, which was about 100 metres across the lawn, when suddenly there was Swami-Ji beside me whispering "I'll race you to the toilet" and off we ran, laughing.

One day I went to him with a very serious question. I was looking deeply at the purpose of my life. Since my brother had taken his own life during a spiritual crisis, I was contemplating the path I was going to continue on and what was important, what was really essential. So I came to my teacher and I asked him, "Swami-Ji, what is my *sadhana*?" *Sadhana* is the Sanskrit word for spiritual practice. "What is my spiritual practice, what are the practices that I should be doing in order to progress on this path of enlightenment?" I was quite blown away by his answer. He said, "Shanti, your *sadhana* is to know who you really are and to be ever eternally joyful".

That was it? To know who I am and to be ever eternally joyful? Wow, I could handle that! I had always somehow known that part of my purpose was to be a spark of joy, of love, and to help ignite that in those around me; he had just confirmed that knowing. By this point in my path I was beginning to recognise an essence in me which was bliss itself, a stillness, a peace inside "which passes all understanding",[5] that peace which is the greatest of all joys. When resting in this fundamental nature, all my cares, worries and concerns would just melt away. I was beginning to recognise this blissful state as my true home, my true nature. That spacious, timeless emptiness that is everything and everywhere – that's who I really am. I realised that it was up to me to be aware of it and choose to live it.

Back in New Zealand (late 1978), I began leading "Sufi dances" and sharing what I had received. Then in early 1980, I was soon to experience the next level of in-depth teaching from life's transformational cauldron. Within a four month period (which for those of you who study astrology was exactly on my Saturn return at 29), I had many powerful experiences: falling off a horse at full gallop and being unable to move for six weeks, my father drowning beside me, having my own near death experience – leaving my body and moving into a realm of light (more later) – as well as completing my legal separation with my first husband. It was an extremely intense time, and an incredible time to spend with my mother and to be there for her and her for me.

At this same time I was studying with a Sufi teacher (Halima McEwan), and she was sharing from the abundance of her life wisdom. I think what was really happening, though, was that I was learning how to listen to my inner guidance and to trust it. What I was soon to realise is that we are being guided all the time. We exist in this luminous field of awareness which is all knowing (omniscient), and omnipresent (as it says in the Bible) as well as omnipotent (all powerful). I finally got it that we are in that field (call it God if you want) all the time and every moment there is guidance coming to us, through us. Now I live my life with an ear to the ground, an ear to the heart… and experience guidance coming from everywhere. The mystery of life has become this exquisite chance to love, to serve and to remember.

Meanwhile, I was living on a beautiful piece of land in the Coromandel, which has now been "home" for almost 35 years. I had more children (with Rainer, who was now my husband), then helped to start a Steiner based school on the land (Tara School) and later co-founded Mana Retreat Centre. Feeling very blessed, I met and did retreats with many teachers like Adyashanti, Gangaji, Ram Das, Richard Moss, Joseph Goldstein and Krishnamurti. But it was life itself that seemed to be really teaching me now after doing the Hakomi training and a sound healing training, having clients and listening deeply to intuition (mine and theirs), facilitating courses and starting to really trust this guidance from within more and more.

In the 1980's I began exploring my path as a woman and got deeply into studying the ancient goddess cultures and archetypes. This really helped me personally with my own journey as a woman and I started facilitating women's groups and working with something that was very close to my heart: empowering women. We often teach what we most need to learn. This was a profound inner journey which began to manifest more outwardly as well. I now have a collection of goddesses from the ancient world. Many are copies of ones that were found in antiquity. Some we sculpted ourselves, talking and laughing as we worked; there was something very primal, intimate and bonding about kneading and moulding clay into the form of earth mothers. These goddesses represent a time when the Divine Feminine was revered: the maiden, mother, matriarch and crone. This exploration helped me to embrace myself fully as a woman and to stand strong in the equality of all beings even while visiting some very patriarchal cultures or feeling the residue of that energy in my own. (See "The Goddess Way".)

When I broke my leg in April 1990 on a retreat that I was co-facilitating, called "The Journey Within", I remember travelling by car to hospital almost an hour away. The pain was very intense; on the body level there was excruciating pain but on another level I felt transported into a blissful space. I felt peaceful in the midst of the cyclone of pain. It was a very powerful experience.

Just a few days before that, I had had another experience with a close friend, Bente. She was telling me that I should do the Reiki (healing touch) training with her. I had no idea if this was something that interested me, as it sounded a bit airy fairy. I love deep massage and it seemed to me that Reiki was not really doing anything. Bente gave me a session so I could experience Reiki for myself and I felt very relaxed, but nothing exceptional seemed to happen. Then afterwards we were sitting having a cup of tea and I looked at her and it was as if I was seeing her higher self. There was a huge golden and multi-layered aura extending about two feet out from her physical body. It was so beautiful. Tears fell from my eyes and we just stayed in that state of wonder for quite some time. I had seen auras before, but this was different, really like seeing the being of light that was her soul self. As you can imagine, I decided to do the three levels of training that Reiki recommends.

Over the years, as I have learned and experienced more about energy and energy fields, I have become aware and much more conscious of the effect that sacred sites can have on us – places that have been built on ley lines (mystical alignments of natural and sacred sites) or ancient goddess sites, or structures that were built in sacred proportions or with a sacred intention. I started to travel to many of these sites and to have strong experiences of energy at some of them.

Probably one of the most profound experiences was in Egypt in 1997, while visiting the island of Philae where there is an ancient Temple of Isis, the goddess of life, childbirth and motherhood. This was a beautiful shrine to Isis where her high priestesses lived in days gone by. As soon as we disembarked from the *fellucca* (boat) and stepped on to the rocky island, I felt a rush of energy inside of me. My heartbeat quickened as we passed through the first archway, dwarfed and overshadowed by its imposing 60-foot (20 metre) towers and by the colonnade of 31 carved columns stretching out before us. For the entire two or three hours we were there I shook, cried, and felt cellular memories of walking, robes flowing, towards the holy of holies: the altar at the very back of the temple. Not on a mind level but on more of a soul level, I knew this place; I knew I had lived there. I had never before had an experience of *déjà vu* as strong as this. I will never forget that feeling. There was no doubt, just a knowing. Egypt, not the pharaoh aspect of Egypt but the ancient goddess times, has had an amazing effect on me. I have been there twice more since then, but that first experience was the strongest. Each time I have said, "This is it, I feel complete", and then something has called me back again. These and experiences like this have been transformative for me. They have opened my eyes to possibilities that I had never dreamed of before.

My travels have taken me to many other sacred sites all over the world: Machu Picchu (the "Lost City of the Incas" high in the Peruvian Andes), and the great Pyramids of Egypt (where we sang in the Kings' and Queens' chambers as well as the pit, after being taken in there at dawn alone with our small group). The temples of the Mayans and Incas. Standing stones around Ireland, Scotland and England, some erected by unknown worshipers over two thousand years BC. Relics buried in caves and enshrined in temples in Burma and Japan with their deep roots in Buddhism. The majestic Himalayan Shangri-La of Bhutan. Cambodia's Angkor Wat, which was hidden in the jungle for over a thousand years – so many amazing ancient sites that bring shivers to the spine. As you come upon Angkor Wat in the forest with huge trees growing out of the temples, or turn a corner and suddenly see the massive Kamakura Buddha in Japan, you can only be filled with awe. Dancing for the Dalai Lama in Dharamsala, meeting with shamans in the Andes – I have been so blessed.

Life just keeps unfolding, and these days gratitude is filling me to overflowing. I feel so grateful for life, for love, for all the beings who have contributed to this beauty and splendour, and for opportunities to share the abundance of this life with whoever comes our way.

I no longer feel that "seeker" energy but more this sense of arriving into each moment and just enjoying what is. That doesn't mean that my journey doesn't take me to all sorts of places and experiences, but I no longer feel driven by that, more just a wonderment at this incredible gift of life and all it has to offer if we are willing to be open to possibilities.

Tools (Practices) for the Journey

Since ancient times there has been this call to awaken, to know who we are. Now in the 21st century there seems to be almost an urgency. It is time to collectively remember who we are and what we came here for. The background of my first teacher – Swami Shyam – is Hindu, but his wisdom and teachings are Universal. He used to say:

We must know ourselves as pure awareness.

The body will change and perish but the inner unseen life will remain. This knowing dissolves the painful glue of separation which is the major cause of our suffering. He said, "Only through dying to the illusion of ourselves as separate from the one reality can we find life everlasting".

We are all different character types; when conditions are right and according to our evolution, we will feel the call to remember. It doesn't matter whether we melt into God through devotion (Sufi leader Hazrat Inayat Khan asked, "Let me be melted in thy divine ocean as a pearl in wine"), or whether we open into the spaciousness through meditation or enter an exalted state while praying or chanting. Many of us call on God to help improve the dream, but what really matters is that we awaken and begin to live and share this awareness.

Swami Shyam spoke of the seven qualities of a free being. He or she:
1. is peaceful;
2. takes life as it comes;
3. speaks and lives the truth;

4. shows order and rhythm in life;

5. gives service to others;

6. has a gentle, kind, forgiving nature; and

7. is humble.

Near the end of the chapter on "Buddhist Principles" is another, sometimes overlapping, list of attributes of an awakening being proposed by Buddha and later teachers in his tradition. The Buddha speaks of the need to nurture the six perfections, which are: generosity, wholesome living, patience, energy, concentration and insight/wisdom. These virtues are paradoxically already part of our true nature, but have often been blotted out by our sense of separation.

Obviously to develop generosity requires giving (see Chapter 6). Giving overcomes greed and "opens the heart" (an expression I use often). To me, opening the heart is the willingness to surrender to what is rather than resisting; it means developing compassion and empathy, accepting others as they are, and imagining what it would be like to walk in their shoes. In the words of Cheryl Strayed,

Compassion isn't about solutions.
It's about giving all the love that you've got. (70)

When we understand others' suffering, it becomes easier to forgive and to support each other. As we cultivate wholesomeness in our lives we become more peaceful and at ease in ourselves. As William Blake wrote in *The Marriage of Heaven and Hell*:

If the doors of perception were cleansed,
Everything would appear... as it is,
[Luminous and] Infinite. (xxii)

As long as we are entrenched in duality our senses confirm our feeling of separation. But once we shift to a recognition of unity, suddenly our senses are doorways to the divine. We hear and see the

One everywhere. Everything is part of a marvellous pulsating whole; one light vibrating through all of existence. Worth waking up for! The method of awakening is simply a tool, not the goal.

Oneness is our natural state of being. What touches you touches me. This is interbeing – we are all part of one luminous field. On this physical level, duality (separation) appears to be what is real, but this is the illusion. To awaken to this truth is the mystical union – the vision of oneness – the One without a second. It could be as easy as a simple shift in consciousness from separation to oneness, *but* how to do that? And once we have had a glimpse of that, then the question is how to hold that, when the appearance of separation seems to be so reinforced on this level of existence.

Obviously, this is the journey.

Along the way there are teachers, books and supportive companions that can aid our unfoldment into what we already are. So why the journey, if we already are that? It seems that light wouldn't know it was light without darkness, oneness wouldn't realise itself without separation. It's the old prodigal son story: the rapture of the lost soul returning home. Ahhh… the joy of reuniting, of consciously knowing our interconnectedness with all of life.

Life provides all of this if we are open and willing (and even if we are not). Perhaps it is a little like sowing a seed. We can till the ground, plant the seed – and the rest just happens, if we continue to tend it and notice what it needs to thrive. All the different traditions offer methods to prepare the ground and care for this growth in consciousness. We each need to gather what fits for us. That might be a matter of culture, conditioning or past life experiences. Some of us may need to choose a path and stay on it for life. Some may take from different paths what serves them at different times. Others may need to receive direct inner guidance and an outer path could be an obstacle. There is no right or wrong way to find God; if we are willing God finds us. The Divine has its ways of seducing us back to our true home. Free will is an incredible gift but it means that there is no pushing – instead we are allowed to bumble along and learn the lessons we need to learn in order to open to unity.

So how do we begin to move towards this state of unity and understanding, which is our birthright, in our all too distracting lives of materialism and forgetfulness? How can we awaken to this remembrance of our essential selves? Let us look briefly at some *tools and practices for the journey*. Some will deserve a deeper look later.

Meditation is an exceptionally helpful practice which also provides down time for the nervous system. It can increase all levels of awareness and help transform habitual emotional thought patterns. Although there are many varieties of meditation, the intention is to bring about greater mental, emotional and spiritual well-being. By turning our awareness within, we become conscious of and attentive to so many other levels of being. We learn to focus and concentrate our attention. This centring can be done in a number of ways, which will be discussed later (Resource 2), but each person must find what suits them. Some may choose to use a mantra to help them enter the inner dimensions, or the breath may be enough, but for others it might be techniques of visualisation, insight and other forms of contemplation.

At different points of your journey you will probably be drawn to different meditation techniques. In the beginning, it is enough to begin to quiet the chattering "monkey mind", the constantly moving and often erratic stream of consciousness that is our usual state,[6] and notice that you can start to observe the mind. If we are to know ourselves, there is no greater tool than meditation. In the end, all of life can become a meditation as we learn to live with awareness and grace.

There are a few practices that can help to cultivate that awareness:

- friendliness to all that arises (Ernst) – welcoming it all: the good, the bad and the ugly;

- inquiry (for example, how would it be to not touch the next thought? And the next?);
- practice being right here;
- notice impermanence (can we let go of our need for things to stay the same?);
- see the suffering of trying to make permanent that which is impermanent;
- notice interbeing and stay connected to wonder, to awe; and
- recognise that we are that spaciousness, boundless and free.

What is the experience like when we don't add anything to it? Just be with it as it is? What would happen if we stopped all this efforting and correction? All meditation practices prepare us just to rest into our true nature – what we already are.

We can spend a lot of time trying to heal ourselves and focusing on our wounds, sorting through all the layers of "stuff". Or we can just sit still, anchored in our heart, and know who we are, embracing it all in that infinite spaciousness. With nothing we need to fix or push away, we can welcome all that arises. The most effective way to heal our past is by living wholeheartedly and fully in the present. It is a radical shift, a decision to let go of clinging to a sense of separate self and suffering and instead to fall into presence, into love.

It can be interesting to notice how our contribution to the world may lie right next to our wound. We are often inspired to serve or to teach what we have learned from these difficult and challenging life lessons.

It is important that we can discern the difference between the impermanent and the permanent. We can see that the body will grow old and perish, relations are changing and the mind is changing. That which is unchanging is often veiled and obscured by the mind's fascination with the changing: how love can turn to hate, joy to sorrow. Unless the knowledge and experience of the eternal is

17

cultivated, we remain caught up in changing external circumstances and experiences and our responses to them.

Meditation offers an opportunity for the mind to be released from all of this and to directly perceive the unchanging underlying awareness. It can be very uncomplicated. One can simply sit quietly and comfortably, closing the eyes and taking a moment to just let the thoughts come and go, to float through like clouds in an empty sky. Rest back into that spaciousness – that sky-like, vast space of awareness – unchanging and ever present. Keep coming home to that. Simply put your attention on the space rather than the thoughts… on the unchanging which lies under all that which is changing. This is our true nature. Just as waves rise and fall into the ocean so do thoughts arise and fall in that space. Put your attention on that oceanic consciousness, the Source of all.

When we come home to this awareness, we find that we are always immersed in this vast shimmering field of consciousness. There is then no need to fight or even resist our thoughts. We can simply breathe and be present. As time goes by our meditation practice can transition seamlessly into mindfulness in everyday life.

Mindfulness means to keep coming home to the present moment. Thich Nhat Hanh teaches that being mindful connects us to our essence. It can improve our ability to stay centred and calm when the mind gets anxious or caught in old painful habit patterns. We can then use this tool to breathe, let go, and use whatever has arisen as an opportunity to practice mindfulness. When we wash the dishes, we can be present to that, feeling the warm water on our hands. When we are with a friend, we can simply be there with them, present and listening deeply. We can be in nature and allow ourselves to really be present to what is without labels or interpretation. Experience a tree or a mountain just as it is, in all its magnificence. If an emotion arises, like sadness, we can just be with it in all its depth. No need to push anything away. As we have probably all noticed, what we resist persists.

For me an awareness of *softening* is really helpful; this sounds like a small thing but it has an immense effect. We can mindfully soften the breath, becoming conscious of different body parts. Allow the teeth to separate and the jaw to relax, and soften the shoulders, belly and knees as well as the mind. This releases tightness and causes energy to flow more fluidly. A lovely Indonesian yoga instructor – Estee – reminds us that all release is good release.[7]

Mindful walking can also be a supportive and nourishing practice, taking the time to walk slowly and peacefully on the earth, breathing in the beauty that surrounds us. We can so easily take moments during our day to pause, breathe, and rest into ourselves. As we open to this level of experience, our sense of separation can fade. This brings such an aliveness to every moment and life becomes a meditation. With mindfulness the ordinary can become extraordinary. All that is required is to show up, slow down and be present. Suddenly the bird sounds can touch us deeply, or the eyes of a loved one. Your presence has power. In fact, this tool is so powerful that you will find much more on mindfulness later.

Breathing Techniques (*Pranayama*). One of the easiest ways to move into a deeper, more open, expanded state is to simply become aware of your breath. Watch what happens when you get into the habit of mindfully breathing before you do or say something.

In Latin, the word *spiritus* means both breath and spirit. They are intricately linked. Breathing is the first and last thing we do as we enter and leave this physical realm. There are many ways to work with breath, including yoga and meditation. Mindful breathing slows down the mind and releases stress and anxiety. It relaxes the body and helps us to centre, especially if we breathe deeply into the *hara* (energy centre or *chakra*) just two inches below the navel. The *hara* is called *dantian* in Chinese, which translates as the "golden light ball". The ancients advise that a strong foundation is needed in this centre in order to grow spiritually, like a tree that has its roots deep into the earth. You can create little rituals during the day, anchors of mindfulness where you simply become aware of breathing.

For those new to *pranayama* please see Resource 3 for some tips on getting started.

Yoga. An ancient practice linking the body and breath with movements, yoga serves to relax and calm the nervous system and open the practitioner to states of peace, bliss and union. In fact, in Sanskrit yoga *means* union: union of body, mind and spirit.

I have been doing yoga since 1973. For me, the benefits have been many. One can experience a sense of serenity while practicing that can become more and more your natural state. Certainly one's body becomes more flexible and toned and there is an overall increase in health and well-being. Simultaneously, yoga improves posture and boosts the immune system. It encourages the practitioner to relax, slow down, breathe deeply and focus on the present moment – all really good things. If living more consciously is something that calls you, yoga can definitely support that. Conscious living, in turn, may help and encourage us to break free of any unskilful[8] or destructive habits in our lives. A regular yoga practice can bring many benefits on all these levels. Why not give it a go? You may never look back.

Singing/Chanting. I am part of a wonderful small choir, as well as a chanting group. For me singing is a hotline to Spirit, one of the simplest ways to uplift my awareness. We can connect with the higher aspect of self either by simple toning and just opening to the sound coming through, or devotional songs that open the heart, or by chanting sacred phrases. There are chants from many traditions. Find ones that speak to you and allow yourself to let go completely into them. Also, when you sing with others you can explore harmonies and let the sound lead you into the unknown, where all kinds of magical things can happen as the mystery reveals itself through you. If this interests you, see Chapter Five on the healing power of sound.

Dance. We were born to move, and to dance is to fully enjoy our embodiment. Dancing allows us to stretch; to feel our bodies alive; to listen to what the body wants and trust that to unfold in its own way; to lose ourselves in the dance, surrendering to the music, exploring all the rhythms and nuances; to empty and be filled. Expressing through dance is one of my great joys. It can be primal, erotic, ecstatic, playful, chaotic and verging on the sublime. You may spin (like the Dervishes, into ecstasy) or surrender into a dance that dances you, or do a more structured type of sacred dance (like the dances of Universal Peace). All these methods have powerful potential for opening and connecting you to deeply divine states. Here at Mana, Geordie Jahner offers a fabulous Tuesday morning dance class called "Open Floor". Check out www.openfloor.co.nz, as it may be happening near you.

Don't think you can learn to sing or dance? A familiar African proverb reminds us that "If you can talk you can sing; if you can walk you can dance".

Prayer, Dedication and Gratitude. We can begin each day with a prayer of gratitude, perhaps asking for guidance or that our actions be for the highest good of all, setting a sacred intention for our day. It is possible to meet each person with kindness and interest, as a gift sent to us by life itself. At the end of the day, we can rest back in the stillness, the presence, and again give thanks. Gratitude creates a lot to be grateful for. It is a real key to joyful wholehearted living. To be aware each day of what we are grateful for is a wonderful practice.

Devotion (*Bhakti*). Our love and devotion to a person or an ideal, or God itself, is a powerful form of transformation, as the grosser self transmutes through the process. When our hearts are open, we are deeply touched, moved by life. For my dear friend Lalita, it is chanting that opens her to this devotional space.

Service (*Karma*). Everything we do can be an offering, a chance to give back to life. We can take the time to nourish life with kindness, offering the gift of our loving presence as a way to express gratitude for this precious gift of life. Susan Conroy, while volunteering with Mother Teresa, learned from her that love is key, but that love alone is not enough; it must be translated into service (81).

Being of service can bring more meaning to our lives and raise our levels of joy. Finding our own particular way to contribute, to serve, to give back to life, brings with it a deep satisfaction and sense of purpose. The Buddha advises that if we light a lamp for someone else, it will brighten our own path. Similarly, an old friend of mine used to say that if we want to be happy in life then find ways to contribute to others' happiness, because the joy we give out comes right back to our own heart. In her book about Mother Teresa, Conroy quoted the late Albert Schweitzer, who went even further:

> *The only ones among you who will be*
> *really happy are those who have sought*
> *and found how to serve.* (132)

Studying (*Gyan*). Each tradition provides a map (teachings) that can help to guide us on our own path or deepen us in our chosen one. As the Sufis say, if the shoe fits, wear it – we each need to find our own way. Studying the various teachings of different traditions, including ancient scriptures, can be helpful and inspiring. For example, Buddhists speak of "The Triple Gem". The first aspect is Buddha himself, or our own Buddha nature. The second aspect is the teachings – the *Dharma* – the way, the vehicle we use on our journey that can help us and serve to ignite our own inner knowing. The third aspect is the community (spiritual companions) which we'll consider in depth later. The Buddha first spoke of four noble truths and the eightfold path (see Chapter Four on "Buddhist Principles"). These are only a very small portion of Buddha's teachings which, like the Bible, *Talmud*, *Vedas*, *Qur'an* and other scriptures, all help to point the way.

Hakomi is a spiritually based, body centred psychotherapy. The work is done in a deeply mindful state so that students learn to observe how they are self organised and run by certain core beliefs. In this mindful state and with the guidance of the therapist, they can allow transformation to occur as they let go of deep-seated beliefs and find new, more skilful ways of being. It has as its foundation five principles: unity consciousness, non-violence (never pushing against the flow), organicity (trusting the process), mindfulness (staying focused in the present moment) and mind/body holism. I have found Hakomi to be an invaluable tool to work with others in a very profound way.

Your Creative Expressions are all ways to channel through the divine energy, by beginning everything you do with the awareness that you are plugged in and totally connected to Source and allowing it to express through you, as you, as much as possible. There are infinite ways to do this. Again, we find what calls us at the time. It can range from something as simple as growing flowers, to more complex arts. Everything we do can take on that quality of spirit in action. Be willing to show your soul in all that you do; the world needs that, longs for that.

Conscious Dying. To live and die consciously is a big undertaking. If we live well, chances are we will die well. Many traditions speak of our moment of death as exceedingly important, worth spending our life preparing for. These bodies are impermanent, and realising the preciousness of this human rebirth encourages us to make the best use of the limited time available. The Buddha has said that everything that has a beginning has an ending. If we make our peace with that, all will be well. These bodies will perish but the Spirit is eternal.

To be able to come to that moment of death (or help others to do so) in a way that allows us to be at peace with our lives and to let go into our infinite nature is a worthy task. In order to do this, we must complete unfinished business, allow healing into our wounded relationships and practice non-clinging awareness now, so that when death calls, we can answer wholeheartedly. It is a powerful gateway from which none of us shall escape – may we have the courage to soar through and to let others go when their time comes.

On the day I die when I'm being carried toward the
grave, don't weep...
The tomb looks like a prison, but it's really release
into union...
Your mouth closes here and immediately opens with a
shout of joy there. (94)

~Rumi

Going on Retreat can be a great gift to yourself, setting aside time that is dedicated specifically to your inner unfoldment. This can be a more organised retreat like a *Vipassana* (where participants will learn or practice *Vipassana* meditation: mindfulness of breathing to gain insights into the nature of reality) or just heading alone into the bush (see some suggestions and contemplations in Resource 4). These times of deep inner reflection can be like a deep well of nourishment for the soul.

Spending Time with a Master can accelerate one's awakening and be extraordinarily inspiring. In our lives we might have many teachers and if we are lucky (blessed, I mean) to encounter a highly evolved or awakened being, a real quickening of our unfoldment is possible.

Such a quickening happens when the aspirant is ready. The teacher appears. In 1974, at 23, I met an awakened being. It was a synchronistic event which guided me to that particular place to meet Swami Shyam in Montreal that day. As soon as I walked into the sunlit room where he sat, surrounded by about ten of his students, I felt a wave of love that was so unconditional my eyes filled with tears. Overwhelmed, I sat bathing in the presence of this love and wisdom. He took my six-month baby Kyla into his arms and continued speaking about things that my whole being was longing to hear; things that I felt like I knew, but somehow was waiting to have them confirmed. He initiated me and took me to a deeper level in my understanding of meditation and how to connect to the Source within. I would never be the same. I longed to spend more time with him and realise in myself what I tasted in him as my potential. He told me I could come and study with him in India, but not for three more years (when my child turned four), but that he would be with me. During those years I did feel guided, as if I was being prepared for some kind of higher initiation.

When I met Swami Shyam again in 1977, my body/mind felt like it let go of layers and layers of "stuff". I sat in front of him in meditation, and when I opened my eyes I was zinging with energy – his eyes were in mine. I felt like I received so much energy through his glance (*darshan*). He beckoned me to come forward, nearer to him; I did, and he touched me. My body went into a sort of spasm (almost like an epileptic fit) releasing deep levels of holding. My identity of who I thought I was seemed to disappear in all this and I was in a deep state of feeling connected to all of life, not separate from anything. He put one of his close followers in charge of me, saying that I would be in this state for three days. He just asked them to care for my body so I would have that freedom, that space to dissolve, and dissolve I did.

He was my main teacher and guide for many years and I learned and unlearned a lot. Mostly I enjoyed having an awakened being as a role model. This is incredibly inspiring and can help cut through the drama of separation straight to the core. However, the role of the outer teacher is simply to awaken the inner teacher and it was Swami-Ji who said, "Once the match is ignited it shouldn't keep sticking to the flint".

Life Itself is a powerful teacher, and we receive many lessons from life along the way. We all grapple with the inevitable vulnerability of being human: the fragility of these bodies and minds as well as the suffering in and around us.

Our suffering can be a major teacher, often showing us the places we are stuck and attached. Since it has often been said that it is our resistance to what is which causes our suffering, another gateway to realisation could be as simple as letting go of resisting what is and instead, practice accepting it. Perhaps even giving thanks for it. When we are simply open to what is, bliss is our natural condition. Every cell is vibrating to that frequency. So as we let go and trust the process of our lives and our inner knowing, that which we are seeking reveals itself. Rumi reminds us that what we are seeking is seeking us.[9]

This is where an awakened teacher can – through their living this state – be a mirror to us of our full potential. However, like Narcissus we must be careful not to get overly attached to the image in the mirror. Instead we can allow it to inspire us to move towards our highest potential, to become our unique and authentic true self, and to know that just as we are, we are worthy of love and that we are the love for which we have been searching. If we notice that certain events or emotional states keep showing up (for example grief or irritation) can we befriend these states? This is our soul work, and life will bring us what we need to grow and evolve.

Spiritual Community

We need to help each other build communities where love is something tangible. "This may be the most important thing we can do for the survival of the Earth" (Thich Nhat Hanh – or Thây – at a discourse in 2005).[10] Most of the renowned spiritual paths speak of the importance of community. In Buddhism it is referred to as the *sangha;* in Christianity, fellowship; in Hinduism, *satsang* etc. They all speak of the value of having like-minded people around us who are also dedicated to unfolding their highest potential and living in an inspired, conscious manner. Rumi recommends that wherever we find ourselves, we "be the soul of that place".

Very often on the spiritual path one can become isolated and cut off from others. There is this paradox of needing to seek that still small voice within, often in solitude, and also wanting kindred spirits to help keep us on track and to remind us of our essential unity. Knowing how to create sacred space in our homes and in our lives can support us to have a place of refuge and stillness to retreat to.

In order for community to contribute to our highest unfoldment it helps to have that as a focus, as an intention. This can be a deeply supportive experience. Jesus said, "For when two or more are gathered in my name, there I am in the midst of them" (Matthew 18:20).

The mystics of old seemed few and far between. Now we are entering an age where many are being called to awaken from all walks of life. The Earth herself is going through such a powerful time of change that we need all hands on deck. We need, however, an enlightened humanity working together for the good of all. Just thinking about one's self, one's family and nation is no longer enough; a sense of unity and an understanding of the interconnectedness of all of life are needed in order to best serve our purpose here and now.

How do we begin to awaken that sense of purpose, that unity consciousness, so that we don't create pockets of isolated mystics, but rather a global family with a vast enough consciousness to hold all of us and our beautiful planet in our loving awareness? Is it possible to live and die consciously, and in between realise our essential unity in the great circle of life?

In my country the Maori have a proverb that the three most important things in life are *Nga Tangata, Nga Tangata, Nga Tangata* (the people, the people, the people). Let us look at some skilful ways of coming together.

Mana Retreat Centre

In our community at Dharma Gaia (dharmagaia.org) and Mana, on the Coromandel Peninsula in New Zealand (Figure 1, manaretreat.com) we have regular meditation gatherings which

Figure 1. Mana Retreat Centre from the garden.

support and encourage each of us to practice mindful, caring, responsible living. We meet and meditate, as well as walking mindfully in silence together along peaceful forest trails. Silence and mindful sharing is a tremendous aid towards awakening. Done together as a community, it is a great unifying factor.

Singing and giving thanks together is an ancient form of inducing ecstasy and can be a real source of connection to Spirit. We have a weekly choir that sings inspired songs in four part harmony as well as exploring sound together. This is a great delight to many of us. It connects us beyond words and often serves to dissolve or transform many issues in an alchemical way, uniting us all in a profound space. We also dance together, another powerful way to connect on a deeper level.

When there were primary-school-aged children among us, we built an alternative school in the bush by a stream. Our two youngest attended this Waldorf/Steiner based school. Tara School also served as a hub for us all to come together to celebrate festivals that marked the turning of the seasons and honoured our connection to Spirit. Its structure was later expanded and converted into the Dharma Gaia Centre for Mindful Living.

At Mana, we come together to garden, learn skills and share massage and tools like tai chi or yoga, or to make music and to communicate on a deeper level. Obviously in any community one has to be watchful of gravitating towards gossip, back-biting or judging others. If this shadow aspect can be minimised through awareness, understanding and loving kindness, there are great possibilities for moving closer together and creating a supportive energy that can be such a blessing. I often see it as a spiral starting with the self then extending to the family, then the community, then to the whole planet. If we look at the word community we see it speaks of our common unity: that which unites us. If we all can try to honour the diversity which we bring to a group yet hold the unity – the place where we are interconnected – then much is possible.

Figure 2. View from Tara Sanctuary.

In western culture the church (Figure 2) is often the central focus of a community. Its steeple can be seen from far off, reaching up to the heavens, calling us to worship. In our community we have built Tara Sanctuary as a place of prayer, meditation, singing and services. For me this is the real soul of Mana. It is exquisitely beautiful, and from its bell tower the bells ring down the valley calling us to remember to pause, breathe and momentarily let go of worldly cares. Every cell can hear the call to awaken.

Resource 5 contains Mana's mission statement, vision and some guiding principles.

Other Spiritual Centres

In the study of community and its capacity to unite us in a shared higher purpose, it can be very helpful to visit established communities such as Taizé – a Christian based community in France, begun in 1945 by the late Brother Roger. This is a pilgrimage spot for many who journey there from all over the world. According to their website (www.taize.fr/en), it swells in numbers to over 4,000 during the summer period. The focus is on worship through song and prayer. I find that the daily rhythm provides one with a time of deep inner reflection, combined with community service and rejoicing through song, and we make the pilgrimage as often as we can.

Plum village, also in France, is a community where people practice mindful compassionate living based on Buddhist teachings and inspired by Thich Nhat Hanh (a well known Vietnamese Zen Master). It is a fourfold *sangha*: monks, nuns and resident lay friends (both men and women) live there full time. Retreats are offered year around. We stayed there twice, for two weeks each time, during their summer retreats. Thây gave a discourse almost every day. He works with coming home to yourself, to the present moment, with the support of mindful breathing, deep listening and many of the other Buddhist principles. He is a very beautiful, gentle and enlightened being, and we were so blessed to meet him and to have that time in his presence.

It is said that the coming of Christ could be the coming of the spirit of Christ within community (i.e. Rudolf Steiner (1861-1925) in his lecture series *The Reappearance of Christ in the Etheric*). Within a community, we can begin to let go of our more selfish separative identification and instead ask questions like: "Will this benefit the group and produce unity? Will this be for the highest good of all?" Helping to create an enlightened planetary civilisation becomes a real possibility, where the reality of our shared and common unity begins to flourish and grow.

The Bodhisattva Vow

These techniques can inspire and ignite us on our way but it is important not to get overly attached to the method. As Buddhist wisdom expresses this, once we've crossed the river we don't need to keep carrying the raft on our back. Once we find ourselves at one with the living principles (like the six perfections outlined in Chapter 4), we can let go of any technique that helped us to re-realise this state. This is who we really are, our true abode, so we don't need to keep efforting. All that is required is to open to what is; to be that which we are. Once the veil of illusion (of separation) is removed, this reality shines forth unhindered.

There are so many paradoxes on the spiritual path. For example, without effort and discipline, nothing is achieved, yet effort can get in our way and become an obstacle. Can we find that effortless ease where there is no need to force anything and no need to hold anything back either? A teacher can be a huge inspiration and source of guidance, yet in the ninth century the founder of the *Rinzai* sect (Chan Master Linji) said, "If you meet the Buddha – kill him!" This extreme expression indicates the importance of not getting caught up or too reliant on certain dogma, rituals or second-hand knowledge. In other words, we have to be able to let go of all our attachments, living in the world yet not of it. One of our highest intentions can be the vow of the *bodhisattva* to awaken for the sake of all beings. Here is Tarchin Hearn's version of the *bodhisattva* vow from *Daily Puja*:

> *However innumerable beings are,*
> *I vow to meet them with kindness and interest.*
> *However inexhaustible the states of suffering are,*
> *I vow to touch them with patience and love.*
> *However immeasurable the Dharmas are,*
> *I vow to explore them deeply.*
> *However incomparable the mystery of interbeing,*
> *I vow to surrender to it freely.*
> *From this day forth, with Wisdom and*
> *Compassion as my Lamp and Staff,*
> *I dedicate all my life energies to the welfare [and*
> *awakening] of all beings.* (7)

It becomes clear that we are here to awaken. As we individually and collectively commit towards living more consciously and deliberately, we shift to a higher level. We become aware that all things are connected in this incredible web of life. This then calls forth a responsibility in us – an ability to respond.

So… let us stand strong together, honouring our interbeing and caring for our planet and each other in a way that reflects our unity and honours our diversity. At this point, what else is there to do?

Obstacles on the Journey

Let us become aware of what obscures our calm, clarity and contentment. Life is short and we want to bring our best to every moment. Any obstacles we encounter can help point out areas of learning we may need to attend to in our lives.

Probably the greatest hindrance is our belief in a separate self, or as the Buddhists call it, the self-cherishing "I". If this state of unity is one thing, it is the releasing of this sense of separation. This separative way of viewing is also the major cause of our suffering. It is this ignorance (ignoring of the truth) which again and again drags us into our deepest pain.

We may get caught in our need to be right, or our need to have things a certain way, or our need to be perfect or to know it all. We may be bound by our cravings for certain substances, or our aversions or intolerance to certain people. (See also the Five Hindrances in Chapter 4.) Whatever is our particular set of obstacles, awareness is always the key. As soon as we become aware of where we are stuck and what is going on, we are already moving towards freedom.

We often get caught in our dramas, thinking them to be so important. This may mean trying to make lots of money so we can possess yet another device, or struggling with trying to find the "perfect relationship". That's a good one (see Chapter 3). All our different bodies can become obstacles if we over-identify with them: i.e. the physical or the emotional body (if we get stuck in our dramas time after time). The mental body can be an obstacle, if we think this is who we are, and put our intellect on a pedestal, substituting knowledge for wisdom and intuition. Why not explore the wisdom of "I don't know"? It can be delightfully freeing to not need to know.

If "having" is the goal, having too much or having too little can both be a form of bondage. Gratefully accepting what is can open us to the abundance that is possible on this level.

All kinds of negative attitudes can become a block to our progress. As we complain, gossip, nag, procrastinate, envy or explode in anger, we sink into the mud of separation. The beauty of our true nature is nowhere to be seen. Although it is normal to have negative feelings arise, it is how we deal with them that matters most. However, Peace Pilgrim said, "If you realized how powerful your thoughts are, you would never think another single negative thought" (15). Being fanatically pious or over indulgent – again all these extreme modes of behaviour can be traps. Even our ideas of freedom can bind us. If it is freedom you are searching for, ask yourself, where am I not free? Where do I feel imprisoned? Can you claim that freedom from the inside out? It's always a choice. Our inner attitude can free us even when our outer circumstances seem to enslave us.

I have heard that once[11] there were two monks returning to their monastery after a day of work in the fields. It had been raining hard and there were big puddles everywhere. At one such place there was a beautiful young woman, unable to cross the deep puddle of water to get to where she needed to go. The elder monk lifted her up and took her across and then continued on his way to the monastery. Later that day the younger monk, fuming, came to the older one and said "Sir, as monks we are not allowed to touch a woman". The elder one acknowledged that this was true and smiling he added, "Brother, I left her on the other side of the road but you are still carrying her".

This story exemplifies how our need for things to be a certain way can often be an obstacle. The middle way has much wisdom, balance and flexibility, allowing us to enter each moment with a willingness to see and to feel what is appropriate and what is being asked for. All the virtues we try so hard to develop are actually within us already. It's just that we have become so overshadowed by our conditioning that our behaviour patterns and strategies reinforce our sense of separation and obstruct our true nature.

Our world is a mirror where Spirit can be seen, heard, felt, tasted – everywhere. Our sense of separation can cause us to miss this. We label something (seeing it separate from us / from the whole), then we no longer experience it as it is – we experience its label. The wise ones see everything as part of themselves. Most people see themselves living in the world; the mystics see the world living in them.

Swami Shyam said, "Most people think if they get what they want they will be happy; the sage knows that the spiritual law works in reverse: be happy and everything you need will come towards you".

He would always say to put your attention on the space, rather than the form. Your way of seeing will change, becoming more light-infused. As you shift to the vision of oneness you begin to experience one vast field of awareness in which you are immersed. Swami used to say, "Begin the path by realising not this, not this, until you are ready to embrace the oneness: *Tat Tvam Asi* – All This is That".

How does one make that shift? It's a bit like a radio station that is just slightly off the channel and distorted, then you turn the dial and there it is clear as a bell. A simple shift of perception is required. If this shift can be balanced by supportive practices like meditation and the imbibing of mystical teachings, this can help a lot; again awareness is the key.

In *Esoteric Psychology*, Alice Bailey wrote:

> *Humanity is a treasure-house of God. Divinity must be lived, expressed and manifested, to be understood. God must be loved, known and revealed within the human heart... in order to be... grasped.* (312)

We can act as transmitters (power houses) for this sacred energy to move through, anchoring the energy here on Earth. We must see ourselves first and foremost as the divine souls that we are. Yes, we are manifesting in earthly bodies, but this is the illusion if we think that is who we really are. We are the meeting ground of heaven and earth, "the word... made flesh" (Bible, John 1:14). In order to begin to live this we just need to realise it consciously rather than waiting to be perfect; we can start where we are. We are a multidimensional happening; this is the miraculous revelation of being human. How do we operate out of all these levels and still remember our divine connectedness? We have come here to awaken within this earthly dimension and to remember who we really are. Then the task becomes calling the rest of our brothers and sisters to that remembrance. It doesn't matter how long we've been asleep, what matters is that we awaken.

It is clear that the easiest way to remove darkness is to bring in the light. So often we try only to work with the darkness, thinking that we can throw it out, when what is often necessary is to just bring in the light. But how to do that, when we are caught up in our own darkness – our troubles and problems? On that level it is very often extremely difficult to "know" what to do, there is so much turbulence. Clarity is not to be found on that level. One must go deeper, past all the layers of "stuff" to the centre. Here there is stillness and a deep peace. This is our refuge, our inner sanctuary. When we connect with this inner space (our essential self) and stay anchored in it, trauma can be released, allowing healing to happen. In that stillness of the heart all returns home, and then our actions can be truly harmonious and clear.

Be still, and know that I am God…

~Bible, Psalm 46:10

Confusion arises when there is a discrepancy between what we know we should do and what we think we should do. On the mind and emotional level there are so many possibilities, but when we connect with the Source within, the path is clear and step by step it unfolds. Rumi reminds us to "move [from] within, but don't move the way fear" wants you to (20).

We are all part of this divine dance. We are all in the flow, in the stream of life, whether we know it or not. As we open our hearts to that truth we learn to be love rather than always waiting for it to come from others. Every moment we need to realise that we have a choice – to react from our old patterns or to respond from our inner knowing. When we choose this we begin to know true freedom, released from the bondage of our conditioned responses and from our sense of a separate self. As this is swept away, there is a natural joy that rises from within. Then we can experience our wholeness and the love that we are. But in order to really be in touch with this space, we need to allow some stillness to seep into our lives. It has been said by many (including Thich Nhat Hanh) that "the way out is in".

Put your attention on the unchanging reality: the space behind all these eternally changing phenomena. All form is nothing but the formless Spirit appearing in its more condensed manifestation – matter. When we are able to see that one reality everywhere, we begin to know the truth that will set us free. Perhaps we are as much in eternity now as we will ever be? Now is all there is. When we understand this it helps to dissolve the glue of attachment to past or future and allows us to be just here, now, with what is.

On our path to knowing the Self, there are many revelations along the way: insights that aid the awakening process, thoughts that inspire.

Life would like us to participate so deeply…
Every moment life can become more and more beautiful…
A peak experience, and by and by,
When we become attuned to the peak that becomes our
abode. [12]

"The journey is the goal" is a saying which has stayed as a reminder for me whenever I get overly goal orientated – to be content with the journey.

You can feel yourself only when you are moving up current.
If you move with the river you cannot feel yourself, you
will feel the river and sooner or later you will become the
river. [13]

We live in a world that is filled with suffering, fear and isolation. These are all expressions of a deep sense of separation rather than unity. It is up to each one of us to explore deeply why we are here and who we really are. Each of us can make a huge difference by living from a place of peace and love. We are all connected on the deepest level; each person who awakens causes a wave of energy in the collective consciousness. These days with our understanding of the holographic nature of the universe we can see how each loving thought, every peaceful response is registered and affects the whole, shifting everything to a more harmonic level. In the same way every angry separative thought is also having its effect.

So as responsible human beings we can support one another to move towards our highest potential, coming to know the truth of interbeing which connects all of life, and recognising our connection to the all-pervading Spirit that vibrates through all of creation. Can we make the shift that is required, allowing thoughts of separation to fall away? This can be encouraged by resting back, trusting the process of our life to unfold, and being willing to step fearlessly into the unknown. Our resistance is our fear, our grasping at limited identities, and yet this seems to be the norm.

According to modern Buddhist scholars such as Whalen Lai, since at least the seventh century, Chinese Buddhists have used the metaphor of the pure Buddha mind as a mirror from which we must diligently wipe the dust of defilement. The Christian tradition as well speaks of how death wipes the dust from the mirror and we can then remember who we truly are.

*For now we see in a mirror dimly, but then face to face;
now I know in part, but then I will know fully just as I
also have been fully known.*

~Bible, 1 Cor. 13:12

The 15th century mystic Kabir, whose poetry inspired Hindus and Muslims alike, urged us not to delay our search for the truth (Kabir's "Guest"). All the ancients tell us that now – while in this body – this is the time to wake up. The effect of this realisation on ourselves, our families, our communities and our planet could be awesome.

> *Friend, hope for the Guest while you are alive.*
> *Jump into experience while you are alive!*
> *Think... and think... while you are alive.*
> *What you call "salvation" belongs to the time before death.*
> *If you don't break your ropes while you're alive,*
> *do you think*
> *ghosts will do it after?*
> *The idea that the soul will join with the ecstatic*
> *just because the body is rotten --*
> *that is all fantasy.*
> *What is found now is found then.*
> *If you find nothing now,*
> *you will simply end up with an apartment in the City of*
> *Death.*
> *If you make love with the divine now, in the next life you*
> *will have the face of satisfied desire. (8)[i]*

It has often been said that the last obstacle or veil is spiritual pride,[14] the desire to be seen as (or the belief that we are) enlightened and special because of our piety or good works. When that falls away we can then see everything as it is, luminous and connected.

Universal Steps on the Path

For some there is a calling, an inner beckoning. For others it can take courage or desperate necessity to get to the point in our lives where we choose to wake up, a willingness to touch our vulnerability, to break free and to burst into the light. It doesn't matter how we begin;

---

[i] From "Kabir: Ecstatic Poems" by Robert Bly. Copyright © 2004 by Robert Bly. Reprinted by permission of Beacon Press, Boston.

what matters is that we do. There are as many paths to awakening as there are beings, yet those enlightened ones who have gone before us can help point the way. Many of these ancient paths are tried and true. Some of the steps such as meditation and prayer are pretty basic to all of them. Other steps found on many paths are:

- taking the time to cultivate our inner life, making that a priority;
- having a meditation practice that suits our own particular nature;
- becoming aware of what helps us to connect with our inner being and nurturing those practices in our lives;
- cultivating gratitude: the Bible recommends, "in every thing give thanks" (1 Thess. 5:18);
- creating space for grace to touch us, whether through walking quietly in nature, or swimming in the ocean or sitting with closed eyes, chanting sacred phrases or praying; and
- finding our own route to realisation and allowing our essential self to flourish and grow.

Equally of value is to be aware of what is not beneficial in our lives and to weed out the things and activities which hinder our unfoldment. Let us not deny what is not working in our lives, yet put our focus mainly on what *is* working, finding creative solutions for our challenges. We can move out of reactivity towards creativity.

The major concept that binds us to our suffering is our sense of separation. To really see this as the misperception it is and to open to the wonder of interbeing is a transformative road. It is always our choice – this is the gift of free will we have all been given. It is up to us to change our thought processes. We can continue to blame everything on our past, our parents, or whatever; but the sooner we take the responsibility of creating an enlightened mind into our own hands, the better. We can let go of all that – it is up to us. We have this amazing opportunity if we will just take it. Life is calling us to the feast of awakening. Why settle for anything less?

CHAPTER TWO: FINDING THE STILL POINT

How do we find the still point, that point where self-conscious thought ceases and we are radiantly at one with the universe? Harold Coward sees this as the ideal of perfection in a number of religions. In both Hinduism and Buddhism, at the still point we are left with "pure consciousness", which Coward likens to "an unrippled mountain lake" in Hinduism and "a constantly moving mountain stream" in Buddhism, both "perfectly reflecting" what is (2). Coward is inspired by and quotes "Burnt Norton" by T.S. Eliot, who was Christian:

At the still point of the turning world. Neither flesh nor fleshless;
Neither from nor towards; at the still point, there the dance is… (2)

One of the questions in Resource 6 may provide a start for your path towards that still point.

All Things are Connected

My children grew up with me reminding them that all life is sacred and connected. After a lifetime of investigation, my key understanding now, and a source of my joy, is the conviction that all things are interconnected. This can be most truly known at the still point.

The ancients have talked about *Samsara* as the wheel of birth, death and rebirth to be released from in order to reach *Nirvana* or liberation, but according to Mahayana Buddhism, the reality is that *Samsara* is *Nirvana* (O'Brien). All This *is* That. It is only our idea of separateness, this mind of ours that thinks duality thoughts (e.g. this is good, that is bad), and it is that illusion of separateness that binds us to our suffering. This is a tree, this is a flower. Quantum physicists describe the universe as being made up of elementary particles and energy, which can be converted one to the other. It is actually all one energy field, appearing as all the different forms. According to Andy Zubko, Albert Einstein said that *"everything is emptiness and form is simply condensed emptiness"* (335). In the *Heart Sutra*, Buddha says the same thing.

Form is emptiness, emptiness is form.

Everything is made of the same stuff, nothing is separate from the Great Infinite Oneness some call God. We all share that longing to belong and yet the innermost self is one and we all belong to that, all of life does. As Joel Goldsmith (1892-1964), founder of the "Infinite Way", explains in *Conscious Union with God*:

It is all God appearing as...

When the Hindus speak of this level being *Maya* (illusion), they don't mean that it doesn't exist. The illusion is in how we view it. Since the One is appearing as the many, if we take the many to be all separate realities, this is illusion: a false way of seeing. This is where we humans so often get stuck in the appearance of things and fail to see the truth.

Let us remind ourselves that God (the Source) is appearing as my partner, my child, my boss, my friend and my irritating associate. That awareness can help us to shift our attitude and treat them with the courtesy and respect with which we would want to be treated. This is the transformative power of knowing who we truly are, and who everyone else is. This is the light of knowledge, the jewel in the heart of the lotus. When we're in nature it is easy to recognise this. The song of the birds, the wind in the trees, the grass swaying, everything is so obviously connected. It's when we're immersed in our everyday lives that we need to be alert. All of these are connected and part of the whole: every being that appears before us is existence appearing as... love appearing as... How would it change the way we related to each other if we were able to stay aware of the diversity but keep our primary focus on the whole? This holistic way of seeing things and being with life can allow us to open to and commune with the current of energy (life force) which connects us to all of life.

We've conjured up so many different names and definitions for the One, and often we get caught up in these labels. Now even the word "God" can upset some people. So then we can just substitute life, or love, or existence, or Source, or Great Spirit, or pure consciousness, or the All. It doesn't matter because it is beyond all names and yet it is. It is everything, and there is nothing apart from that. The moment we are in the now, we are at one with this mystery, this truth. The present moment is timeless. Now is not in time, it is time that is happening in the now. Being in the present moment frees us from the tyranny of time; we are in time and yet beyond time (in the timeless) simultaneously. This is the great mystery. The mind cannot grasp it but the heart knows it.

How much more easily and joyfully we could live our lives if we really understood the basic truth that everything is connected. The Pre-Christian Hindu scriptures (the *Vedas*) state "All This is That".

Brahma is everything. Buddha taught that *there is no independent self.* Thich Nhat Hanh also told us that everything relies on everything else, comes from everything else and returns to everything else. These trees, they came from the earth, they are the earth reaching towards the sky, and they are the sky. They contain all the elements (as do we): earth, water, fire, and air. It is that unknown, intangible, nameless substance or energy that is the life of all that is. Without that life force, the body just returns to the elements.

What if all beings could recognise that and live their lives in accordance with that? We see the awareness of our inter-connectedness emerging in various disguises: recycling, caring for the Earth. But to really understand it — how would that transform the way we live? How would I live differently? How would you live differently? What if we really got it, that everything is connected, nothing is separate from you, from me, nothing separate from God, from life. The sound of that bird sings of it, my heart beats because of it. When we know that, when we live that, everything comes into harmony. This is the kind of harmony that a cat instinctively has, or a tree — any being that exists here without this busy mind that we human beings have. And yet we have allowed ourselves to be taken over by the mind and we have become identified with it, rather than just using it as the incredible tool that it is for working on this level, for recognising this from that. How wondrous it would be if we could just immerse ourselves in the great silence, the great emptiness, the spaciousness, which very quickly reveals itself to be our true nature. Swami Shyam used to always remind us,

Put your attention on the Space.

What a revelation that was for me, because when I closed my eyes in those early days of meditation, there were so many thoughts, so many things that wanted to grab my attention. But when he said "put your attention on the space, on the spaciousness", that was the guiding light that I needed, because the space was always there, always forever free, undying, unchanging, but I had forgotten that. I'd ignored it, because the clutter was somehow noisier, more obvious. The more I put my attention on the space, the louder and clearer it became. I found that the inner space has a sound, a wondrous sound that I could only compare to crickets and cicadas or a buzzing bee, an inner hum. When I deeply listened to it, I saw that the same essence of sound is everywhere, inside and out. It was the sound of the All, as above so below. It was the sound of the universe; it was what the ancients called the *Aum*, Sufis called the *Hu*. It became a beacon for me, a touchstone, and a guiding force. (See the chapter on "The Healing Power of Sound".)

This wonderful poem by Chinese Imperial Librarian Lao-Tzu from the *Tao Te Ching* has spoken to me deeply over the years:

> *Empty yourself of everything.*
> *Let the mind rest at peace.*
> *The ten thousand things rise and fall*
> *While [Awareness] watches their return...*
> *Returning to the Source is stillness,*
> *Which is the way of nature...*

Nature is absolutely connected and in harmony with its Source. The trees, the flowers, the animals, they're just being what they are. It's only us who have somehow lost that harmony, that suchness, of just being with life as it is. We often label or judge things and people and we can be overly concerned with what others think.

How are we different after enlightenment? Capra attributes this legendary answer to the ninth century Ch'an Master Po-Chang Huai-hai: "When hungry, eat, when tired, sleep". Outwardly, life will go on much as usual, except we will live it effortlessly, in the moment, inwardly restored to our original Buddha nature. That is Zen.

I have heard that once, in the time of the Buddha, a disciple asked his master, "What's the difference between you and I?" and the master said "Well no difference really, except you see yourself to be in the world and I know the world is in me". It's that tiny shift of knowing ourselves to be part of all of life and then life can live itself, as us. Not even through us. We are life, we are always plugged into the Source because we are Source, and every bit of us comes from and returns to Source. I wonder why we miss the obvious, even when we've heard it. It seems to me that we must just mistake this small mind for who we are, or this body, or even these emotions. And yet all these are just our vehicles of expression, they're not who we ultimately are. What a joy it is to really know who we are, what a freedom to not have to limit ourselves to such smallness. To wake every day and be surprised. To ask, "Well, how does the universe want to be today?" And then find out. We go through our day and it's filled with surprises, magical surprises, synchronistic events, bursts of joy, tears of sadness, whatever.

So simple, so all inclusive and so liberating. I'm not separate from anything, therefore I don't have to push away or grab hold of anything; I can just be with things as they are.

A really lovely contemplation when out walking in nature, shared with me by Tarchin Hearn, is from "Deep Healing":

> *We experience our intimate connection with all living beings. Breathing in, – gifts from the green plants. Breathing out, – gifts to the green plants. Feeling the moisture in our bodies and knowing that it was once a cloud, a drop of rain, a snow field, and a tear. Breathing with a deepening sense of gratitude and connection. We are all parts of a living earth.*

This is a helpful remembrance of the interconnectedness and interdependence of all of life. We breathe in the oxygen we need from the green plants and then offer back to them the carbon dioxide they need. I sometimes like to add to this the remembrance that I am walking on a living being. It changes the way I walk, brings in a gratitude, a reverence, a smile to my lips, as I feel my body moving through space. Everything seems to slow down as one walks with this kind of awareness. All seems somehow right with the world when we open to the interconnectedness of all of life.

I absolutely trust the wisdom of the universe and its creative Source. We are all connected in that unified field: a field of pure being, pure love, pure intelligence and pure awareness. It is interesting to think back to when we were four or 18 or 30, and now for myself at 65, and realise that essence has always been the same. That inner stillness, that beingness, is always within us, shining. If we take the time to become aware, that shimmering presence is always right here.

Thomas Merton (1915-1968) saw light everywhere:

[We] are all walking around shining like the sun. (155)

When the inner eye is open there is not so much focus on the form but our attention is drawn back to the formless, to the light. Every moment can be made glorious by this light of love.

The 14th Dalai Lama is such a beautiful being. I have had the incredible privilege of holding his hand twice in this lifetime. Once was in India during a photo shoot after we had danced the Tara Dance for him. I felt high and energised for days after that and very, very blessed. He speaks sometimes with shocking simplicity. He said to us, "The purpose of life is to be happy". Can you imagine how our world would be if everyone actually got that? We can let that joy, that love, guide us. That Knower, that knowingness. Swami-Ji always used to say that the purpose of life is to realise the Self. These two statements aren't contradictory to me; they both speak to my heart and to my inner knowing. His meditation instructions to new people were always simple. Close your eyes, watch that space (that spaciousness). Any thoughts that come arise out of that space, they return to that space. Just like waves rise and fall in the ocean so do thoughts rise and fall in that space. Put your attention on that space. That space you are.

After one such meditation in 1995, I wrote:

Dissolving, edges gone,
Molecules dancing,
Nothing solid.
An interconnectedness so deep
That nothing escapes it.

Certainly with a supportive environment awakening can unfold more easily, but the spirit is strong, it can unfold anywhere. This is the Shangri-La: the union that we've all been longing for. This is the Promised Land right here; nowhere we have to get to, nothing else we have to become. What a relief that is, what an incredible recognition. We've always just wanted to be ourselves and that is actually all that we need to be. Sometimes it's hard because we've been conditioned and pushed to try to be something other than we are, or to think that who we are isn't good enough. But at some point we will get the chance to see through that, even for a moment. Who we are is enough, more than enough. We're connected to everything, we're part of everything. Kabir says:

All know that the drop [or the wave] merges into the Ocean
but few know that the Ocean merges into the drop [or the
wave]. (77)

Life and Death at the Still Point

Death is not extinguishing the light;
It is putting out the lamp
because a new dawn has come. (Tagore 174)

Every age is different, with its own challenges and gifts. As we get older, we have the potential to become elders, wisdom holders, capable of being an inspiration and a guiding light for others. We may experience a shift in energy as the inner realms call more and more to us. Albert Einstein expressed this, "I live in that solitude which is painful in youth but delicious in the years of maturity". Becoming an elder means to be more fully oneself, and to discover how we can best be of service and share our gifts and wisdom. Rather than collapsing into old age, we can find real meaning and depth in our lives. Shortly after my father's passing my mother wrote, "I have learned that every chapter must have an ending in our book of life, and one must have the strength and faith to turn the page".

I wanted to talk a bit about death. Each one of us has experienced loss in our lives. I love this saying from Eckhart Tolle's *Stillness Speaks*:

> *Death is not the opposite of life. Life has no opposite. The opposite of death is birth. Life is eternal.* (103)

Life just is. Still, no matter how awake we are, when someone we love dies, it doesn't mean that we're not going to deeply feel it and experience the immense loss of that person on a physical level. But we can allow it to open us to depths, to other levels. That is its hidden gift.

Rumi said:

> *Grief can be the garden of compassion.*
> *If you keep your heart open through everything, your pain can become your greatest ally in your life's search for love and wisdom.* (197)

I have heard that once a woman came to the Buddha, grieving the loss of her child, whom she had in her arms, and she said, "Buddha, I know you can just give the word and my child will be alive again". And Buddha in all his compassion said, "Yes my dear, but first you must succeed in finding a house, any house that hasn't experienced death and loss in the family". So joyfully she went house to house, house to house. But nowhere was there anyone who hadn't experienced a deep sense of loss. So she came back to the Buddha and she was ready. She said, "Now I understand". She laid her daughter down and was ready to grieve, to let go and to move on.

I think death for me has been such a transformative catalyst in my life, such a force for awakening – for finding the still point. We can let the awareness of death remind us to stay awake rather than threaten us and cause us to shut down.

When I was in my early twenties, my brother chose to take his own life in the midst of a spiritual crisis. I was with him in the last few months of his life, trying to convince him not to do it. In the end he did it anyway. I was there that day...

The Hollow Sound

That day in May
We woke at dawn to the hollow empty sound
of the woodpecker.
We walked, our last walk.
Who was to know
You would never see another day.
We sat awhile
Like the lake
Silent and still.
You seemed weary.
You told me you felt the suffering of the world
Burning like a fire inside you.
I guess you already knew.
That afternoon
We found you,
Your body hanging limp
From the tree.
We surrounded you
With love,
The ground wet

With our tears.
Mother wailing.
Father, quiet in his pain.
I said goodbye.
And then, I heard it...
The hollow empty sound
of the woodpecker.

~Shanti, "Picking Up the Pieces"

Amazingly, after that he appeared to me three times. I remember the night just after he died, I was quite uneasy in myself, realising I was a bit afraid he might come to me. Then in all his love and compassion he didn't. But on the third day after he had left his body he appeared to me in meditation, an inner vision. He was this radiant being of light, wrapped in a blanket, not looking entirely like himself. My brother always had an amazing sense of humour. He looked at me and said, "I'd like to extend my condolences for the loss of your brother". Then I felt my eyes start to twinkle in recognition and I said to him, "Yes, but I know he's in good hands". He smiled at me and I smiled at him, and feeling the love that was there flowing between us, I somehow knew that all was well. Then in my young exuberance I turned to tell my family, "Bob's here!" When I turned back he was just dissolving molecules, and then all that was left was a little blue dot that a chipmunk was pawing the air at. That was the first time and it brought both me and my mother a gift, because she always listened to me. What a blessing that was to have a mother who listened. Perhaps she didn't always believe or understand me, but she always listened.

It was three months later when Bob appeared again. I was in Edmonton, Canada, just before returning to New Zealand, and strangely enough I was with two other Bobs. Just before my brother passed he had said, "I'd just like to ask two things of you. The first one is to sing my songs" and he said that he'd be with me when I sang his songs. And the other was "Keep your womb open because if

I come back I'd like to come back through you". So those were his two requests. At the time, he didn't have many possessions. He had a guitar, a songbook, a poncho and a straw hat, and he told me, with his sense of humour which was always very alive, "I know you've had your eye on my hat and my poncho, so you can have them". Anyway, so here we were sitting together, the two other Bobs and me, singing one of my brother Bob's songs, and I was singing my heart out. I was looking at Bob G. and suddenly everything went black and misty, like dissolving molecules, and Bob G. just dissolved, disappeared. Then there sitting in his place was my brother smiling at me and singing. We sang that song together, and somehow it was the most natural thing. Then the song finished and my brother just dissolved into light molecules and there was Bob G. as if nothing had happened, and I guess, on some level, nothing did happen really. It was another profound kind of message from my brother that nothing ever really dies.

The last time my brother came to me, other than in dreams and visions, was after he had been gone three years, in 1979. I was over at somebody's house and they had a visitor I had never met before: Elizabeth. She came up to me and said, "Look, there's somebody tall, red hair, who wants to get a message to you. Do you want to come back later when all these people are gone so I can deliver that?" I knew it was my brother. So I came back a couple of hours later and sure enough, he had a message for me. I don't remember all the details now, I only remember really that he wanted me to know all was well, and the best thing I could do was live my life to the fullest, enjoy life, and that that would bring him immense joy. There was a deep knowing that everything was as it was somehow meant to be.

When my brother passed, it was my father who found him hanging from a tree just behind our cottage. Just moments after he was gone my dad was drawn there. He told me later that whenever he closed his eyes, he saw that image of my brother hanging there. And that was quite a torture for him, as you can imagine, as a father.

When my brother was alive he really wanted my dad to learn how to meditate and my dad was quite resistant. Then after Bob died, my dad studied and practiced some meditation to help himself deal with that image of my brother. Life is strange sometimes, isn't it?

About four years after Bob had passed, my parents were visiting me in New Zealand for the first time, on a holiday. I was living at Waikawau Bay in an old farm house. There were a lot of synchronistic events that led up to what was about to happen.

I should first tell you a bit about my father. At 59, he was still tall and fit, with rather stern Nordic good looks. He was reserved, and although rumour had it that as a young man he was an adventurer, a WWII flying ace, and a jazz musician known as Hot Lips for his prowess on the sax, it was hard for us to imagine. Since becoming a father he had fitted himself into the mould of protector, head of the family, and authoritative military leader.

My father had just come back with my mother from a stunning walk on the Milford track in the South Island, and was over the moon with the beauty and the serenity he had experienced on that trek. I was pleased, because his spirits had been low since my brother's death, and he didn't have the release of talking about it. That day, he felt the clearest, emptiest and the most present that I had seen him in a long time, and he really wanted to go for a swim in the ocean. I wanted to have a cup of tea first but no, he was pushing for this swim. So off we went. He took his shoes off and put his sunglasses in them. I was startled because as a child I always loved to be barefoot and he was always reprimanding me to put my shoes on. And there he was taking his shoes off, running along the sun-baked sand, holding my hand, which I don't remember him doing since I was about six years old.

Laughing, we ran into the ocean, into the waves, and almost immediately there was this sense that the sand had been taken from under us and I heard my dad next to me saying "Oh my God", as if he already somehow knew that this was it. Neither of us knew at that time how to deal with riptides. I found out later that you either just surrender and let it take you until you get to a place where you're out of it, or you swim sideways because the rip isn't very wide. We didn't know any of those things at the time, so we did what was most instinctual and tried desperately with all our strength to swim in towards the shore. In doing that, with the huge waves and the powerful force underneath us, it didn't take very long until we were exhausted, swallowing water and drowning. I tried a few times to communicate with my dad, grabbed his hand, and then there was this profound moment where I saw him die – surrender and let go.

Only a few moments later I felt myself leaving the body and I have to say it was the most wondrous, ecstatic experience. Suddenly there was no more struggle, there was just light and a glorious sound as if the whole universe was singing hallelujah. It was like I was entering the body of God. I can't really describe it, only that there was such magnificence, joy and a profound letting go, but not even letting go anymore, merging with the whole of the universe and the universe was absolutely blissful. Since I had spent the years before that studying Hinduism, Buddhism and Sufism, later when I thought about it, it did come as a surprise to me that somehow I felt the presence of the Christ, but I guess that's just how it is, that was my experience, my heritage. As I just merged with that, all sense of personal self gone, suddenly I was thrown up on the shore. I guess when I surrendered, I must have been thrown out of the rip.

My mother, who hadn't heard us because the roaring ocean was even louder than our screams, saw me and her eyes filled with fear. I yelled to her, "Mom, Dad is dead, he got taken out by a rip". Her first impulse was to immediately run into the ocean; she didn't believe it, she wanted to find and save him. I grabbed onto her really hard and shook her and said, "Mom, you cannot go in there. I've just lost one parent and I'm not going to take a chance on losing another". Still unbelieving, she told me to run for help, a helicopter or whatever I could get. I made her promise not to go in the water and I started to run. It was about a mile to the nearest farm house, and it was as if there was no me, there was just running, this incredible energy running me. I was still connected to an inner state of unity, actually the sense of a separate self had not returned yet, so there was just running.

When I came back with the farmer and another neighbour, on a tractor, my mom was already by the side of the ocean, on the beach, wailing and giving mouth to mouth to my dead father who had also been thrown up on the shore. It was obvious that he was no longer alive. This neighbour, whom I had never met before, was just so kind and compassionate. He said, "Let me take over", and for about ten minutes he did mouth to mouth to what was obviously a dead man, out of the kindness of his heart for my mother. I sometimes see him working on the road now, thirty years later, and there's just a smile that passes between us. We put my father's body on the back of the tractor and I tenderly held my mother, who was shaking and in severe shock. We went to this man's house and there was his wife, pregnant, almost due, and I put my hand on her belly, all of us baffled by the mystery that one soul had just left and another was soon to arrive. We took my father's body inside the house and we all prayed together over it, until the hearse came to take the body away. That evening I could hear my mom crying in the next room, and I remember going and crawling into bed with her. We held each other through that long and unbelievable night.

I never saw that couple again until about two years later. We were driving from Colville to Waikawau Bay, where my father had passed away, when we ran into them. It turned out it was that same neighbour, whom I hadn't seen since he had been giving mouth to mouth resuscitation to my dead father, now giving mouth to mouth to his two year old child. Such synchronicity…this time I was able to let him gently know, "The baby is dead", to pray with him and to cry with him. I had noticed that there was a doctor just around the corner so I was able to give that information to him. The interconnectedness of everything can be astounding sometimes, mind blowing really.

Both my father's and my brother's passing happened in my twenties, and these two tragic experiences were such an awakening for me, propelling me on my journey. Beyond the mind is this essence, this spaciousness, this all pervading energy, that can neither be born nor die but just is everywhere. I had to grow into that knowing, had to take it on and live it, which is never easy. But I have never lost that knowing. So I thank my brother for that, I thank my father for that, and I thank the All that is for that. At such a young age to recognise this essence was a gift. There is a song I often sing by Bruce Cockburn: his message is that all else is transient but "Joy Will Find a Way". Everything changes; everything comes and goes: every thought, every feeling, and every state. But amidst all that impermanence, we can find the changeless, that which just is, the all pervading energy, our Source, our core. Touching on that, knowing that, our lives become free – free to experience the comings and the goings, without needing everything to stay the same way, without holding on or pushing away, without grasping, without aversion. I guess that's the real freedom.

I am thinking about death today…that to die is just to transform. A cloud doesn't "die", it simply changes, transforms into something else. It changes into rain, or into vegetables, or flowers. If the seed you plant doesn't die or transform, how can the tree be born?

"Late Fragment" was the last poem in Raymond Carver's final book *From a New Path to the Waterfall*, written in his late 40's when he was terminally ill with cancer.

And did you get what you wanted from this life, even so?
I did.
And what did you want?
To call myself beloved, to feel myself beloved on the earth.

Singh tells us that Guru Nanak (1469-1539), Sikh founder and considered a saint by Tibet Buddhists, spoke of imagining a world where we saw everything as sacred and connected unconditionally. To live this is to be a beacon of peace and to allow that inner knowing to guide us. With that kind of understanding comes such gratitude and such humbleness.

It helps to begin our day from that place of peace. How about being known for our kindness or our generous heart rather than our titles or our roles? What would you like to be remembered for?

Shanti's Musings

On Self / No Self

The Buddhist lama, the Venerable Kalu Rinpoche (1905-1989), was born in Tibet but his monastery was in Sonada, Darjeeling, India. John Amodeo quoted him in the *Yoga Journal* as follows:

> *You live in illusion and the appearance of things.*
> *There is a Reality. You are that Reality.*
> *When you understand this, you will see that you are*
> *Nothing*
> *And being Nothing you are Everything.* (42)

What a liberating realisation. If we really understand that we are nothing, that we are empty of a separate independent self, then we are also free to realise that we are a part of everything. Just as the wave, when it stops thinking of itself as only a wave, then knows itself to be the vast ocean. When we "live in illusion and the appearance of things" it truly looks as if everything is separate, the forms really do appear that way. Yet when we come to know the underlying reality of all that is, then we can unfold the vision of oneness that sees life as it is: a connected field that excludes nothing and includes everything. We are that which is unborn, undying and all permeating. In deep meditation we can come to know that.

Have you ever had one of those moments where everything seems to be shimmering with light, translucent, where boundaries disappear and instead of focusing on the form, you see dancing, dissolving molecules of light? Or seen auras, energy fields that seem more real than the form they surround? Have you ever allowed yourself to just look at someone or something with soft eyes gazing into infinity through them? If you have, you have probably seen energy fields of light and even incredible colours around them, and/or their faces in flux where many different faces can seem to pulsate and transform; or the face may even dissolve into molecules of light. It is a great privilege to experience this with another being and to recognise they are much more (and much less) than you imagined. If there is no one in your life with whom you feel comfortable exploring this, then try it looking into (and through) your own eyes in a mirror. It takes a few moments to shift from focusing on the form to looking through the form into infinity, but it is worth it. Again remember, put your attention on the space, the formless.

The monkey mind will try to lure us into its dramas and schemes, but we can always bring our awareness home again. The breath is a wonderful tool to again and again call us home. It is not a coincidence that in a number of languages the word for breath and spirit is the same. While we are in these bodies the breath is a profound link to Spirit, to our Source. So whenever the mind tries to cover up the space, we can bring our awareness to simply breathing in and breathing out. This opens up the space again and we can very quickly return to that stillness within.

I have heard that once a Japanese Zen master was serving tea to a university professor who came to inquire about Zen. He poured his visitor's cup full and then just kept on pouring. The professor watched this until he could no longer restrain himself. "Stop... Can't you see that my cup is full? No more can go in!" The master smiled and replied that, "Like this cup you are so full of your opinions and ideas. I can not show you Zen until you empty your cup". When we think we already know, when we are just waiting for our turn to speak and when we are full of facts and speculations, we miss the chance to really receive the wisdom that is being offered as a gift.

Last week I lay in the long grass with my grandchildren watching clouds float by. Oh let us not forget the importance and delight of these moments. Wonder ignites in the heart and all is well. Everything appears luminous. Life is full of these precious moments; we must be careful and alert not to miss them.

Another truth was introduced to me when I was a child by my grandfather, Dr. R.G. Ferguson, who was a great inspiration in my life. He was made an honorary chief and medicine man, presented with a magnificent feather headdress, and given the Cree name Chief Muskeke-O-Kemacan (Great White Physician) by the tribes in his area of Canada. This expression of gratitude for his life of service eradicating tuberculosis meant more to him than any other, even the Order of the British Empire. He used to remind us that,

The only constant thing is change.

All is impermanent, yet there is no need to despair, as the source of all is eternal. I didn't quite understand it then but now I realise that impermanence is not to be feared; it's a great friend. It allows everything to be recycled and renewed and to know that *this too will pass*. I guess my initial resistance to this insight was, if everything is impermanent, it would certainly include me and everything I hold dear. It includes health, youth, joy and all the people I love. Then I recognised later that it also includes illness, old age, sorrow, grief and anger. So in the end I realised, what a gift. Everything comes, everything goes. These experiences, they just happen and I'm free to enjoy them, or not, to let them go, or not. I'm free to be stuck; I'm free to be free. I can be truth, love, whatever I choose to dance with. The more aware I become, the more I have chosen to dance with freedom, joy and love, spaciousness and emptiness. Why not... why not? It has been said that you can either try to fix the dream, or you can just wake up. Stay stuck in the dream or wake up. We can easily forget that wakefulness, not be aware of it, sometimes totally oblivious to this amazing energy that's always here available in us, as us. If we wake up, we can know the dream just as a dream.

We begin by letting go of everything we put after the "I am", everything extra, all our identities and all our thoughts about ourselves, when we come to understand that "form is emptiness, emptiness is form"; "All This is That". Everything is the one energy: the one Spirit, appearing as, dancing as, loving as, being as, dying as. Then we can live our lives with this knowledge, this freedom, which was always our true nature. This joy, this ease, this wonder, with nothing we need to resist or push away. We can allow all these experiences when we don't take them so personally. We can just be with them, bless them, open to them and not need to judge or try to fix them. What a gift to be able to experience this precious life with that kind of awareness and freedom. That's our birthright; that's what we're all unfolding towards. Waking up is a choice, one we can make in each moment.

According to Stephens, when Suzuki Roshi (1904-1971), who founded the first Buddhist monastery in North America, was asked to condense the Buddha's teachings into just a few words, he chose the following.

Everything changes. (34)

Later we can come to know that space which is changeless; that enduring reality which always is behind all that changes. Put your attention on That, you are That.

Just as a cloud can obscure the sky, our identification with mind can obscure that space, that truth of who we really are, but it is always there. This realisation removes the dust from the mirror. That which we are is always present; we have just forgotten. Layer by layer is removed and freedom is experienced. It has nothing to do with the mind. We can recognise our unchanging centre which is pure consciousness and always free. This pure presence *is* our true self. If we only identify with our body, mind or life situation we can lose awareness of our true nature. The invitation is to come home to ourselves.

Breathing out we can surrender fully and completely into that. Breathing in we can receive that presence totally. In *Guided Meditations*, Levine puts it this way:

Watch breath, soften belly, open heart. (85)

Life is a mystery to be lived rather than a problem to be solved. There *is* no one to wake up, there is just awakening; there is no thinker, there is just thinking; there is no walker, there is just walking. So really how we see ourselves is usually all the overlays, like parenthood or our profession, our nationality: all these add-ons. And then we get to the point in our lives where we want to awaken, where we look towards some enlightenment, some lightening up. Then we see that all that we built up over the years, all those identities, we need to actually let them all go. That doesn't mean that we don't keep doing those activities, being a mother or a musician or whatever, but we're no longer defined by them. When we look really deeply there's no one home, there's just beingness, just isness, just a profound presence that is everywhere, a vast field of awareness; nothing very personal about that. The one who knows and lives this truth is free. The illusion of a personal self can be dropped, released. This is only possible through the recognition of the true self. It has been said that the seeing of the real causes the disappearance of the unreal.

Just as a potter knows that all her various cups, plates and vases are all clay, know that all forms are the formless one reality. Buddha called it "No Self"; the 15th century Hindu Brahmin Ramanand called it "The Self".

Reality just is... it is our thoughts, ideas, and judgements about it that make us suffer. We can explore letting things just be as they are. The suffering is often the resistance, the tightness around wanting things to be different than they are, or the stories that we tell ourselves that form our perception of the world. If we then think this is truth, we suffer.

Your thoughts are just thoughts,
Unless you believe them,
They have no power over you.
Otherwise they are just a story.
There is no such thing as a true thought.

~Adyashanti (*Falling Into Grace*)

The excerpt below from "The Master" is attributed to the proverbial sage Ashtavakra by an anonymous master of the school of Hindu philosopher Adi Shankara in Byrom's *The Heart of Awareness: a Translation of the Ashtavakra Gita.*

He has no "I,"
He has no "mine,"
And he shines!
He sees that the Self never suffers or dies.... (65)

You need never get bound or stuck by anything if you know "that space" which you are. If you come to know there is no division, no matter what is going on you can hold that space, that peace, that knowing. Let things be as they are and you will be at peace. When you come to know the Source, it showers the grace. The struggle is optional.

I have heard that once while wandering through the wilderness a young man stumbled on a ferocious tiger that chased him to the edge of a steep cliff. The man leaped in order to try and save himself and grabbed a vine as he tumbled down the cliff. The tiger was above. As the man hung there, two mice appeared and started gnawing at the vine. Then out the corner of his eye the man spotted a juicy fresh wild strawberry. He plucked it and popped it into his mouth. It was absolutely delicious.

Living in the present can turn a disastrous moment into something miraculous and delightful, even if it might be our last. We can enjoy it to the fullest, even when there is no tiger in the room. Let us ask ourselves, are we living our lives wholeheartedly? If so, how wonderful. If not, what attitude might we need to shift so that we can?

You wake up in the morning and fall into the small house of the mind, when the vast sky space within you awaits.

~Swami Shyam

Again from Swami Shyam, a very simple lesson but one that's somehow always been very profound:

Take it as it comes.

In other words we don't have to plan, prepare for all the possibilities or worry about them; we just take it as it comes. The energy will be there for us. Think of how much energy and time human beings spend on their anxieties and worries, instead of allowing the spirit within us to show us the way. In the end it usually does anyway, if we're listening and sometimes even when we're not. Goldie Knight cautions that:

You do not realize that worry is really praying for what you don't want. (128)

Again I remind myself that "the journey is the goal". There's no big goal to reach; certainly not enlightenment, not when we really see that enlightenment is our true nature. We just have to come home; we just have to let go of all that masquerades as self and step into our true selves. In that spaciousness we can enjoy just being, and in that being we find we are a unique expression of the One and we have each been given gifts, passions and joys to share. I know for me I love to sing, to dance, to walk in nature. I love to share with beloveds, to travel and experience this amazing planet. What brings you alive?

What a gift to come home to oneself. It's actually a gift to the whole world, because each of us who comes home, each of us who can live from that place of ease, joy and spaciousness, just being who we are, inspires whoever we come into contact with. Then that inspiration ripples out from us and has definite impact. It goes out in all directions – our freedom and our wakefulness. "Shanti, know who you are and be ever eternally joyful". That brings a smile to my lips. What a wonderful task. What an amazing practice. It also helps to seek out what magnifies our soul, to follow that and to trust that. This allows grace to unfold. I think of it as a sacred responsibility to bring more joy into this troubled world. Every day, who can we lift up, where can we commit random acts of kindness? This is the real peace work; done on a daily basis, it has a substantial effect.

Tarchin Hearn, one of my Buddhist friends and a teacher associated with the Auckland Sphere Group, has written in *Daily Puja*:

> *Frequently I pause*
> *Mindfully I breathe*
> *Simplicity, Openness, Clarity,*
> *Connection and Caring*
> *flowering forth. (13)*

As you move through life, you begin to see more and more that the magical surprises, the greatest teachings, are often hidden in the most unusual and obscure places, sometimes disguised as disastrous situations. I look back on my own life and I see that some of my greatest learnings came out of these very challenging places, especially in the early days; I seemed to need big dramas to wake me up. Now I don't feel a need for those more traumatic happenings, yet knowing how much I learned from them helps me through the many times when I'd like to interfere with things that are going on in other peoples' lives or run to the rescue of one of my four children. It stops me, allows me to breathe and say well, who knows? Who knows where their lives need to take them right now? Who knows what they need to learn? Who knows what they might teach later? This may be their doorway. Certainly my brother's death was a huge doorway for me, an immensely transformative experience. Those wounds that break our hearts also open us and can be gateways to new levels of compassion and understanding, softening and unlocking our hearts to more intimate connections with life and those we love. "*Sarva mangalam*"[15] is an ancient Tibetan saying which translates as "All is blessing".

Whatever is happening – it's raining, it's storming, it's hot, it's cold – it's just as it is, we don't have to bring in our judgements of good and bad, our ideas of right and wrong, our dualistic way of looking at things. We often have such a small comfort zone of maybe twenty-two degrees and anything under that is too cold and anything above that is too hot. When we take things as they are, as they come, there is so much more potential for enjoyment and gratitude. The wind just is: powerful, enlivening; the rain just is: soft, moisturising the earth; the heat: melting us down so that all we want to do is sit under a tree and enjoy. If we don't resist life, we can just be with what is, just as it is. It's this incredible smorgasbord of experiences. If we get in touch with that space, devoid of a separate judging self, and can just be with these passing experiences, then they can be fully experienced, savoured and even cherished. Another one of my favourite sayings from the Buddha:

Suffering is simply resistance to what is.

Whenever we find ourselves resisting, suffering is just around the corner. Whenever we find ourselves suffering, if we look deeply we'll see that we're resisting something. It doesn't mean that there's not pain. Of course there's pain, it comes with having a body, but suffering is optional.

Over my adult life (after I met Swami-Ji in 1974), I went many times to Kullu, to be in his presence and to keep alive the flame that was burning within me. The community there would come together as a group almost every day to share *satsang*. Swami would remind us in many different ways that we usually think that the Self (presence), is in the body but actually the body is in the Self. That we think we are in the world but actually the world is in us. A whole shift of perspective is required to be in the company of a free being. I realised that I am a multileveled being, not just this body and mind. Yes, I have a body that changes *and* I am life unchanging/everlasting. To come to know the unchanging can be truly liberating.

Most human beings take birth and forget their true nature. Behind the thinking, underneath the emotions, who am I? This is what we have come here to remember. We have never actually been separate from this, we have just forgotten. That which is invisible is so easily forgotten whereas the visible appears to be what is real. The reality that connects us all is invisible but true.

Last time I was at the ashram in Kullu, I asked a number of the people who had been living there for years what they felt was the fruit of their *sadhana* (their practice) and how had this knowledge transformed the way they live their lives? One woman answered that she doesn't suffer anymore. That doesn't mean she isn't in pain sometimes but that she doesn't choose to resist and therefore suffer.

Swami would remind us that our commitment to him was never to divide or separate as this would cause us to be miserable. He was a voice calling us home. He would say that someone had to tell us that our belief in a separate self is just not true. That the deepest truth is that we are unbound and free at the core, in our essence, so this essence needs to be revealed. Usually it is covered and obscured by our conditioning from the world around us. It is important to see the places that we are hooked and need to unhook. To bring our attention to these stuck places in ourselves with a willingness to touch them with love and tenderness so that we are able to move on. Are we willing to set aside the habits that are not serving us? Can we become a finely tuned instrument for joy for those around us, and can we be quick to apologise if we have hurt someone in any way? Where can we be more grateful? Appreciative of all those around us who bless our lives with their presence? It is a human tendency to focus on what is not working (the problem). How about shifting our focus to being grateful for what *is* working? We could explore falling in love with the miracle of existence rather than focusing on our complaints and our stories, which can be never ending. Can we soften our desire for things to need to be a certain way? Can we live more fully, more wholeheartedly, daring to express our natural beauty? We only need to watch a hawk in flight, a cat about to pounce to know that we creatures are meant to be fully alive and embodied. My voice teacher Ruth Weimer reminds me, "*Dare more*".

Guidance

If we listen deeply we will find that we are receiving guidance all the time. It is a very powerful insight to realise that we are always in "the field". In other words, we are never apart from God/Spirit/Source. When we truly "get" this we begin to see that guidance is coming from all sides, within and without. Everything is connected to everything else in the field. I find I need a piece of paper handy to write on during the day and at night. Some guidance just jumps into me and I know I need to do this, phone that person, connect with another etc. Guidance doesn't niggle us in the way our obsessive thoughts can – often it just comes and then leaves us. After all, we have been given the gift of free will. Nothing is mandatory. But if we want to be in the zone, in the flow of life, then we can follow the clues that are being given to us every day, and life begins to unfold in a more than magical way with synchronicities in abundance. You are texting someone and they are ringing you at the same time; just what you need falls in your lap. We all know that feeling of being in the zone, but this multiplies amazingly when we are listening deeply to our inner knowing and acting on it. Following these synchronicities and trusting the process is part of guidance: we can lean into life and let ourselves be guided by our inner knowing as well as trusting what our heart delights in.

Morgan quotes Japanese Rinzai Zen Master Bankei Yōtaku (1622-1693), who reminds us:

Everything is perfectly managed in the unborn. (195)

As I say this, it's starting to rain as I walk. Part of that perfect management is listening to our inner voice. Just as I set off on this walk my inner knowing had me grab an umbrella even though the sun was shining. The more we can be empty, the more space there is actually to hear and trust our inner knowing.

I was talking to my son Sasha about two major disasters that happened when he was together with some friends. Both times just before it happened he said that he had a knowing, an intuition. The emptier we are the more we can hear and pay attention to the universal mind, the big mind that our little mind is part of. It's only when the little mind is overwhelmed with all our personal dramas that we sometimes don't hear the messages that are coming to us. Just as a flower knows the day is coming to an end, and it's time to close its petals, there are so many things like that which we just know, that just come to us, not necessarily as a thought but more like a cellular knowing. It may be as a thought, sometimes even as a voice, sometimes as a feeling. What a wondrous thing it is to be guided by these inner knowings that are not outside of us, they're right here. The Monarch butterfly knows when it's time to migrate, the geese know when and where to go. We have that same knowingness. All we have to do is open to it, give it space, and listen to it. "Everything is perfectly managed in the unborn". Can we take our hands off the steering wheel (metaphorically speaking)? Can we let go of our need to control and to manage things? Can we just allow things to be the way they are: magical, surprising, unknown?

Trust is a very important aspect of guidance, but of course we need to be clear on where and in what we put our trust.

I have heard that once there was a sufi master crossing the desert with his disciple. When they arrived at an inn late one night, the disciple, who was responsible for their camel, was exhausted. Instead of tying up the camel, he just prayed to Allah to watch over it. In the morning, the camel was gone. The master asked his disciple what had become of it. The disciple replied that he had no idea, but that he was not responsible – the master was always telling him to trust in Allah, and that's what he had done. The Master then replied, "Trust in Allah but tether your camel first".

Once he had done all he could – and tied up the camel – then the rest could be left in God's hands. If we give our best to life, that is our part. Then if we can accept whatever happens, we will find a peace and contentment as well as an ease and lightness which will be a blessing to ourselves and those around us.

I have to share a little story. About forty years ago I was living in Maui for a few months and in those days I had very little, only what I could carry on my back, and because I had a child to carry as well that wasn't much. We were invited to go walking out in the desert into the dormant Haleakala Crater, and the man who was inviting us looked at my bare feet and said, "But you'll need to wear some shoes". Mine had just fallen apart and I didn't have the money to buy new ones, but I just pictured in my mind's eye these shoes, designed exactly as I wanted, the perfect shoe. I hadn't told anybody about the shoes that I had envisioned. That night I was sleeping in a tent with my daughter and partner, camped behind a sandbank on an isolated beach by the ocean. I got up to pee and there sitting against the tent were these shoes. They looked just like the ones I had imagined that afternoon. I tried them on and they fit me like a glove. I put my hands up in the air and said, "Hallelujah!" and gave thanks. I called them my magic shoes and I had them for years until I passed them on to a friend who needed a little magic in her life at the time. "Everything is perfectly managed in the unborn". Not everything happens as magically as that, but every once in a while we get those sorts of astonishing happenings in life that bring us to our knees in gratitude, in amazement. I'm sure all of us have experienced some of these miraculous moments.

These stories that happen in our lives can be like fingers pointing to the moon: they can serve as sign posts. I think this is all that a good teacher is ever wanting or trying to be. I think Jesus and Buddha used stories (parables) to help in the awakening process, because sometimes these stories can jolt us out of our everyday way of being into the unknown, into the mystery, into that place where we're awestruck. This is an awesome universe we live in where there are miracles happening every day. We just have to stay alert for them, stay tuned and open to the miraculous. Remember, your true nature is one with the nature of God.

The real miracle is that everything is connected; everything is plugged into the same knowingness that guides the All. So the more we can get out of our own way and stay plugged into that great mystery, the more amazing our lives will be.

It's really only fear that can get in our way. What are we afraid of? Of being all that we are? Of being happy? Of dying? Maybe the death of our separate self is seen by the mind as very scary, a deep letting go. It's so important not to let our fear keep us from being courageous and really alive. Opening our arms and hearts wide to life with all its joys and sorrows; that is living on the edge. The title of Susan Jeffers' book expresses this well:

Feel the Fear... and Do It Anyway.

I remember my mother saying to me once, "You know I'm really shy", and I said, "Well Mum you manage to travel the world, you give lectures in front of groups". She said "Yes, but every time I just push myself to do that, because even stronger than my fear is the fear of my fear stopping me". I thought that was very insightful. It's when we let our fear stop us or take over that it keeps us from being connected to the magic of life, and from being awake to what is. Perhaps courage is just fear that is willing to surrender. Remember, everyone has fear sometimes, but do we let it stop us or energise us? I like to imagine my fear like a veil. I then have a choice to move through it, and when I do I have found an abundance of energy — even excitement — on the other side.

Years ago, in my early twenties, I was studying natural medicine with a man whom I greatly respected and from whom I received a lot of inspirational guidance. Over the few years that I studied with him, I knew him as a very awake and free being. One day I was visiting him, hoping to receive more insightful teachings, when he surprised me immensely by saying that he was no longer teaching, that he had run into a wall of fear and could no longer pretend that he could be a guide to others. I left quite taken aback, and wondering how this was possible for someone with so much wisdom. I was feeling bewildered, and then suddenly out in the cold snowy forest I felt this incredible fear well up in me. I found myself lying in the crisp snow, unable to move, truly "frozen" with fear. This fortunately didn't last too long. Energy arose in me and I was able to get up and move and get to shelter. The universe was teaching me important lessons: that fear can sneak in when we least expect it, and never to judge another for what is actually part of the human condition. I felt so grateful for this teaching and another one I received on transmuting fear. In 1977 my teacher spontaneously asked me to speak about truth to a whole room of seasoned meditators, when I felt like such a novice. I was gripped with panic. He gently but firmly told me to close my eyes for a moment and come home to myself. Then he said, with authority, "*Shanti, there is no one out there but you*". I got it; it landed as truth in my being and I simply opened my eyes and started to speak, and the words flowed into me with ease.

It's raining on me now and I have put down my umbrella. I am enjoying the rain, just as it is. We are surrounded daily by this majesty, this beauty. We only have to lift our heads and look, open our senses and listen, feel, be. Palmo shares a parable in which the Buddha leads an Indian holy man to enlightenment with this teaching:

In the hearing there is [only] the hearing, in the seeing there is [only] the seeing, in the sensing there is [only] the sensing, and in the thinking there is [only] the thinking. (134)

So when we're just with what is, as it is (as for a moment I am just with the wind, the rain) it's pretty simple really, just being mindful. My son Sasha reminds me, "Joy can be found when we are willing to be just with what is right now".

This life is a gift. We don't know how long we're here for, but here we are. In this moment we're right here. It's all we've got for sure, right now. The past is gone, the future hasn't arrived yet, and here we are. We have the chance to be fresh, alive and awake to what is. That doesn't mean that there won't be times when we use this wonderful mind of ours to plan and to prepare for things. But then we use it, instead of it using us all the time. Many indigenous cultures speak of the need for us to show up in our lives (revealing our worth to ourselves and others), to be fully present, to speak our truth and to say what we mean and to do what we say. This way we can give life our best and then let go and surrender the rest to Spirit.

There's something I have been contemplating that Adyashanti said during *satsang* at a retreat in 2005. He compared dealing with thoughts to walking through a crowd. He said, "When you find yourself walking through a crowd, you don't deliberately head towards the people and bump into them, you head towards the spaces. Deal with thoughts in the same way. You don't have to put your attention on the thoughts [the stories], go towards the spaces". Somehow the thoughts then just glide away, float away like clouds in a big blue empty sky, and here you are, awake, present, plugged in, luminous, astounded by the wonder of it all.

Stop looking for answers in the world; no one else can tell you what is right for you. Keep coming back to the centre, the Source, where peace always is. Getting out of the prison of our minds is what spiritual practice is all about. Suffering is caused by what we tell ourselves about what is happening, not necessarily by what is actually happening. Can we let the suffering or pain just be a reminder to ourselves to wake up? Good to bear in mind that our suffering can be toxic to others. We can then take responsibility for what we put out. We must "like a lion breaking its cage, break [our own] chains and be free..."[16]   No one else can do it for us. *Remember, you always have a choice.*

In the *Dhammapada*, as translated by Byrom, the Buddha says:

> *Live in serenity and joy.*
> *The wise [being] delights in the truth*
> *And follows the [path] of the awakened.* (23-24)

* * *

Abiding in the Luminous Heart
A practice offered by Atum (inspired by Padmasambhava)[17]

Begin by taking a few conscious breaths, relaxing into yourself and slowly, with awareness, be deeply with each of these inner reflections. Breathe with them; allow them to penetrate into your core.

- Deeply rooted... in the present moment;
- Seeing from a clear, open spacious mind;
- Beyond doubt and fear;
- Abiding in the Luminous Heart of equanimity;
- The Way unfolds before me.

CHAPTER THREE: THE DANCE OF RELATIONSHIPS

O love, O pure deep love, be here, be now…
Make me your servant, your breath, your core. (368)

~Rumi

In this chapter, we will explore the joy that is possible in mindful, loving relationships. You will find exercises to help build compassion and empathy and to resolve conflicts in our most intimate relationships (present and past). The chapter ends with a section honouring our gender differences.

Mindful Connections / Return to Love

To be mindful is to choose to pay attention without judgement to this moment, just as it is. When we can be truly present for another, love is. That loving presence is the real alchemy. Sanaya Roman explains that "unconditional love" is about *"learning to be the source of love rather than waiting"* for it to come from others (100). *Whatever we reflect out will reflect back at us.* If we offer out loving kindness and joy, that is what will come back to us. Fulfilling relationships involve two whole people who want rather than need to be together, who can complement each other rather than complete each other, and who can enjoy the dance of relationship.

Whether the relationship you want to strengthen is an emotional and sexual one with a partner, your bond with a sibling or child, a dear friendship, or your interbeing with the universe, mindfulness is the key. Mindfulness allows you to fully connect with others, and by definition, a relationship *is* the "the state of being connected".[18] Then it is possible to learn to love like we have never loved before; this is truly a practice worth cultivating.

Loving all, we become love,
Becoming love we find we are deeply loved. ~Shanti

The following was written in 2005, inspired by my time at the monastery in Plum Village, France with Thich Nhat Hanh.

Mindfulness is to be present to each moment, just as it is. Life is really only fully available in the present moment. Presence is the key. If we look into the present moment we also can see our future, as it is a continuation of this moment. If we care for this moment we take care of the future.

Breathing mindfully we can come home, we can arrive right here. We can then turn down our negative channels and instead choose to turn up channels of loving kindness, compassion, joy and forgiveness. These are wholesome activities which will create more of the same. Each moment we are creating imprints which will inform our future moments. If we practice in this way, our lives can become a love story. The path is not to be perfect but just to do our best. When we offer loving kindness and cherish the other person's happiness, they too will flourish. Love is something sacred and precious, something to be savoured and cherished. If we live simply we find we have more time to take care of those we love. This includes ourselves, so that we will be fit and able to care for those who are entrusted to us.

The kingdom of God is at hand in every moment. It is the energy of mindfulness and loving kindness that opens the way for this to unfold. This energy is always available, but are we? Are we truly here and present? Awakening to our true nature is a major work. That is the practice that will bring us home to ourselves in a way that we can then be of service to all those around us. The purpose of life is really to be our own unique self, to feel and know our connection with all of life and to find that vast spaciousness within. It is our task to be fully human beings – no more and no less.

We have the opportunity, dare I say the responsibility, to transmit everything that is beautiful and wholesome within us as our offering back to life in thanksgiving. This happens when we give to life all the beauty and goodness that is within us as well as being able and willing to see the darkness and transform it with our right thinking, right speech and thoughtful actions. *If we want peace we need to be peace.* If we want love we need to be love and to share love.

When suffering arises we can learn how to be with it, how to make compost out of our suffering so that flowers of joy can eventually arise out of it. We can learn how to really be there for another's suffering, to listen deeply and to try to understand.

A wonderful present to offer another on their birthday can be to water the positive seeds that we see in them, appreciating and acknowledging them for their many acts of kindness and all the things that we love and admire about them. The practice of deep listening and loving speech can allow two people to really be together. It can help to practice deep breathing while listening with love and compassion. This can be very healing. Just breathe and be present, staying anchored in the heart. To listen deeply is to love. Here and there we may choose to water wholesome seeds in order to nourish their innate goodness and our own. Offering a friend or partner a chance to experience being really heard is often all that is needed to move on.

Selective watering can mean watering the flowers rather than the garbage. We have both in us. If we are aware of what we water and what we consume we can see that some television programmes can nurture the seeds of anger, fear or violence in us. Before we consume something, be it TV, music, books etc. it helps to look deeply to see if these will be a wholesome consumption for ourselves or our children. Will it support our well-being or will it drag our energy down? It is very beneficial to be mindful of this and to go into things with this kind of awareness. In the same way, if we let ourselves be swept away by worries and fears we can lose our joy. Can we stop and breathe and come back to what is nourishing, and bring joy to this moment?

It can also be helpful to be aware of our parents' short-comings as these same seeds are likely to be in us and in need of transforming, not only for ourselves but for them and for our descendents. It is also beneficial to be aware of their strengths, as those seeds are also in us and need to be watered and cared for.

When anger or fear is making itself known in us or in another, we can simply breathe, feel it, acknowledge it and meet it with kindness, calmness and compassion. When we align with love in this way, our traumas and agendas can simply dissolve. Yet if we meet these with reaction or resistance we will activate them even more. Mindfulness allows us to live without regret. Good intentions are not enough; our habit patterns are strong, and the only way to transform them is with mindfulness. Then we can see our habits as they arise and choose to respond differently. When even just one person walks or talks in mindfulness, they affect everyone.

Our own particular idea of happiness may be an obstacle to true happiness. Can we release our idea of what has to be there for happiness to manifest? Can we allow happiness to come from unknown directions, and be ready to receive it and to open ourselves to it? Can we recognise that as we share joy, it multiplies and expands? We can then begin to feel a sense of inner alignment with the bigger picture, with life, for it is in life that truth is found.

There is no inner happiness without true freedom. Walk/live as a free being. Walk as if you are embracing the Earth with your love, your gentleness. Remember that as you free yourself, you free your ancestors whom you carry within you – every cell of your body contains their DNA. We must stay aware so that we can carry ourselves and our ancestors to freedom. If we walk and breathe and live in such a way, wholeheartedly present and awake, we have the potential to support many other beings to do the same. Interbeing is a reality that shows us our sacred responsibility to live in a way that supports and uplifts the world, our ancestors and our descendents, as well as all beings everywhere.

We can live our life not as a separate self but with an awareness that everything we do affects all of us. Look deeply and you will see the presence of your mother and your father and all your ancestors within you. Know yourself, look within and you will see that you are made up of earth and sky and star dust. Let this inspire you to awaken and to be free. From this space you can respond rather than react. It is the ego that reacts. The soul responds.

The practice of meditation and mindfulness is really about coming back to ourselves to restore inner harmony and peace. Mindfulness is the energy that carries with it concentration, presence, understanding and loving kindness. When we restore the inner harmony in ourselves it is much easier to be of service to another person who may be in need. Caring for ourselves and re-establishing our own inner peace is the basic condition for helping anyone. *If we want to see peace in the world we must first create it in ourselves.*

Once we begin to become more rooted in the energy of mindfulness, and our sense of loving kindness for ourselves and others begins to flourish, it seems to me we have what I can only call a sacred duty to bring our best to life, to each moment; to become more and more aware of the effect that our thoughts, words and actions have on our own lives and the people around us, and ultimately all beings. If we are able to live with kindness, if we are able to offer love and understanding to others, we can make a huge difference in our world. Our lives can become an act of blessing. Every day can be a chance to love and to serve in whatever way is right before us. We do not need to look very far; we can start right where we are. David Loy quotes these insightful lines by Nisargadatta (1897-1981) in *New Buddhist Path*.

When I look inside and I see that I am nothing, that's wisdom.
When I look outside and see that I am everything, that's love.
Between these two my life turns. (54)

So much joy is found in this way of living, and from that joy grows great gratitude, and from that gratitude more joy. *Gratitude is a real key.*

As we become more and more conscious we become aware of wanting to be less and less the cause of suffering to ourselves and to others, and instead to be a source of healing and love. Can we be more a part of the solution instead of the problem? Can we ask ourselves what is needed here?

We all grapple with the fragility of being human but can we shift our focus from what we can be getting out of situations and people to what we can be giving, offering? Ask yourself, "Can I be more generous than I knew myself to be?" We begin to see the incredible joy there is in bringing happiness to others and how little it may take to do that. It is often just a small and simple act of kindness that can touch another deeply and make their day (and it will probably make yours as well). The true joy comes in the giving and sharing of joy. Mother Teresa reminded us that,

If we have no peace [in our lives] it is because we have
forgotten that we belong to each other. (Oman 47)

We can begin to ask ourselves at the end of each day... "What am I grateful for today? Was I able to extend compassion, understanding, tolerance and a generous heart today?" We can begin to surprise ourselves at how much loving is actually possible, and how many kind acts can joyfully fill a day.

I am contemplating the art of living and realising that every moment we are creating a work of art – ourselves! We can create something mediocre or something truly beautiful. It all depends on the qualities that we practice and develop and which ones we don't.

Rainer Maria Rilke (1875-1926) reminds us,

Be lavish with your praise.

Appreciate others, those near and dear to us, those we work with and just anyone who comes our way who touches us with their beautiful and caring presence. He reminds us that any bad-mouthing or gossip not only brings the person being spoken about down, but also ourselves. He says that we can't improve anything with that kind of negativity as it will end up poisoning our cells and others. Often it would be far wiser not to say anything, as some things would be better left unsaid. He reminds us to express that which will uplift rather than that which will drag down. Meister Eckhart wrote,

If the only prayer you said in your entire life was, "thank you," that would suffice.[19]

This is how we can care for our relationships and our world.

Rumi said,

Out beyond our ideas of right and wrong
There is a field,
[A luminous field,]
I'll meet you there. (21)

In that luminous field all opposites fall away, all dualistic ways of thinking. We can truly meet, just as we are. Suddenly problems dissolve of their own accord and solutions appear. Any need to attack or defend is gone as we come face to face with the reality that it was our illusion of separateness that created the problem, or the need to be right. Then, with that understanding, we can let go and meet in that luminous field where things just are as they are. There we find that there is one truth, within and without, which is the essence of all that is. If we know this truth we know ourselves. If we know ourselves we know God. As the illusion of the false self is released, the truth appears, shining and radiant.

In that luminous field there is Love,
And in that Love
The whole universe pours its heart into you. ~ Shanti

I was delighted to hear while in Japan that they don't use a subject and object in their communication; for example, rather than saying "I love you" they say "loving". How freeing is that? Simply loving; with no need to possess. It somehow, for me, honours the recognition that we *are* love; it does not need to be sought in another, but shared with all. Knowing that we are love allows us to stop the desperate search to find love outside ourselves, and instead to rest back into the love that we are. Our natural instinct will then be to share this abundance, for in sharing it the heart just keeps expanding.

What if your sole purpose today was simply to bless
everyone you meet
With your smile, your touch, your words of kindness and
encouragement,
Your presence and your Love? [20]

That changes everything, doesn't it? Instead of being out to get something, accomplish and produce, we are offering the gift of our loving presence wherever we go, bringing blessing to all we come in contact with. Our lives are rich with loving and full of generosity. A generous heart is a joyful heart. Swami-Ji said,

Be a generator of love. Lift others and the world will be lifted.

Stop for a moment right now and just consider, how could you offer love today? We all know (I hope) that loving is contagious, that it is a mushroom-like phenomenon. It is one of the most powerful ways to transform our planet. Begin local and it becomes global, expanding in all directions. You plant a seed of joy in one heart and it can begin to spiral out. Try it. Explore the possibilities of making a huge difference with your loving presence. My mother often advised,

Fill the cracks with love.

Every day there are so many opportunities to "fill the cracks with love". In *Live like a Window Work like a Mirror*, Mark Brown said that we always have a two second gap where we can choose how to respond (rather than react) to any given situation (122). We could ask ourselves, "How would love respond? What would bring more light, more joy into this situation?" We always have a choice. Sometimes we may react unskilfully from our old negative habit patterns *but* we can grab that gap, and make a new, more skilful choice. Each time, each moment that we do that we create more freedom and joy in ourselves and those around us. We can give ourselves (and others) the gift of allowing ourselves to stop mid sentence if we find ourselves speaking harshly, negatively or judgmentally. Interrupting our old negative habit patterns gives them the opportunity to change and us a chance to begin anew, fresh and with more wisdom and skilfulness. When we take a moment to plant a seed of love, everyone blossoms. It is love that unites us and sets us free. Real love gives support to others' growth without making conditions. It is flexible and willing; it accepts others as they are. Rabindranath Tagore wrote,

Love is the only reality... It is the ultimate truth at the heart of creation.

With love comes happiness. Swami Shyam told us,

Be happy and all the reasons to be happy will flood toward you.

He explained that in the world people usually expect or wait for circumstances or people outside of them to make them happy, but the reverse is true. Just be happy from the inside out. Try it, it works!

The Buddha advised us that,

There is no way to happiness, happiness is the way.

One of Thich Nhat Hanh's beautiful reminders is,

Happiness is not an individual matter.

If we are not in a state of acceptance, enjoyment or enthusiasm, then if we look deeply we will find that our resistance is creating suffering for ourselves and for others. Why would we consciously want to do that, one wonders?

What do you become when you are in the presence of love? Are you willing to claim your greatness? To be all that you are? Or do you fall back into old habit patterns and see yourself as small and limited? Our choice... always.

Our deepest fear is not that we are inadequate. Our deepest fear is that we are powerful beyond measure. It is our light, not our darkness that most frightens us... As we're liberated from our own fear, our presence automatically liberates others. (165)

~Marianne Williamson

Are we afraid to be the radiant beings of light that we truly are? Why don't we let our light shine so that we can bring benefit to all we touch and come in contact with? We can then be a generator of love, a powerhouse of well-being. Or are we looking for reassurance? We all need to look at the attention seeking dramas we play and begin just to be at ease in ourselves so that who we really are is free to unfold and to flower. Then we can give all other beings the dignity they deserve. Jesus reminded us not to hide our light "under a bushel", to let it shine "unto all" (Matthew 5:15). Every step we take towards this kind of freedom is a gift to humanity as we evolve together. As Thich Nhat Hanh says, "Freedom is not given to us by anyone, we need to cultivate it in ourselves; this is a daily practice".

You and Your Life Partner

We saw earlier that the effort to find the "perfect relationship" can be an obstacle on our inner journey. So much energy can be spent on looking for the perfect partner or trying to make our partner perfect (instead of accepting them as they are). Or trying to be right (instead of being big enough to see different viewpoints). How about taking a broader view? If we can accept – perhaps even enjoy – our differences, the road of relationships can be much smoother. We so often try to blame someone else for all the unhappiness in our own lives (instead of taking responsibility for creating and enjoying our own life). So we ditch that partner, thinking the next one will be better, only to encounter very similar difficulties once the honeymoon phase is over. In relationships we have the possibility of deeply sharing the playground of life and supporting each other to move towards our highest potential. We may embrace each other's (and our own) shadow in a way that will allow much to dissolve and to integrate. Relationship is a powerful tool and grow from it we will. If we are willing, so much is possible.

There is no need to deny what isn't working in our lives or in our relationships, but an ease and lightness can arise when we focus more on what *is* working. Then we can become shape shifters, able to find creative solutions to our challenges. We can move from reactivity towards creativity.

Movement is growth. It is so important not to put each other in a box and think we know that person or even ourselves. Everyone is a living mystery, and we can enjoy a lifetime of exploring that together if we are open and make a conscious decision not to label and judge one another, but to give each other (and everyone) the freedom and space to grow and change. Everyone yearns for that depth of acknowledgement and understanding but it is a rare gift to give another.

There are many ways that we can support our relationship to thrive and to bring out the best in each other, such as:

- spending quality time together every day even if it is only fifteen minutes;
- taking the time to:
  o listen attentively to each other's feelings, challenges and insights;
  o appreciate one another;
  o create space for spontaneous moments of affection;
  o celebrate milestones; and
  o find moments of stillness and peace;
- sharing adventures and laughter; and
- exercising and relaxing together. Perhaps consider sharing a meditation or yoga practice or learn to dance together?

These special times together diffuse tension and open the way for more easily managing conflict when it arises.

Nothing grows us and transforms us like love. This tribute to love from *Heaven on Earth* (published by Penguin) is by Stephanie Dowrick, adapted by her from *The Universal Heart*, and reproduced with her permission.

There is no other way to love but generously.
Love treasures who you are.
Love brings depth and joy to the life
You are continuously creating.

Love opens you to all that you can do and be.
Love makes it easy to receive.
Love lives through acts and actions:
kindness, respect, delight, trust, safety.

Love finds what's good and speaks of it.
Love knows what to overlook.
And the value of silence.

Love laughs loudly and often.
Love is daring as well as kind.
Love seeks and offers beauty.
Love is subtle and discerning.

Love thinks easily of others.
Love listens with an open mind.
Love is loyal and respectful.
Love gives thanks and is thankful.

Love honours freedom.
Love does not cling.
Love seeks to understand.
In love, there are no opponents.
Love wishes the best for the other, always.
And even when it is afraid of the answer,
love asks what the best might be.

Love brings quiet patience.
Love makes things right.
Love affirms difference and diversity.
Love makes you vulnerable.
Love mends wounded hearts.

Love belongs to no one and to everyone.
Love lets bad times pass and treasures good times.
Loves brings you into the present moment.
Love is a commitment and a calling.
Love never dies. (181-182)

On Marriage

As a registered marriage celebrant, I officiate at weddings, and help to prepare couples for that important step. I wrote this for one of the weddings I did in the Sanctuary at Mana.

Love is a Wondrous Thing

Love is probably the most marvellous quality that we can bring to our lives. Let us contemplate together, for a moment, the miracle of love and the mysterious weavings of this tapestry of life. Marriage begins with a willingness to make a commitment to do what it takes to grow and deepen together. For in truly learning to love and accept another human being as they are, we can learn to love and accept ourselves and potentially all of humanity. This is the healing power of love.

Today you are promising to water seeds of love in the difficult times as well as the good, and you will be transformed by these commitments. Commitment is a sustained energy in a particular direction. Needless to say this "sustained energy" is of great importance as we need to continuously nourish our relationship to keep it alive and vibrant. We need to guard our commitment to each other so that the love and the trust between us can deepen. Then, over the years our love can become a very precious treasure.

In *Letters to a Young Poet*, Rainer Maria Rilke also suggests that we need to *guard each other's solitude*. This is a beautiful image. When we both recognise each others' need for inner reflection and alone time we can be guardians for each other. Every human being has a deep longing for freedom, and this must be nourished alongside our desire to love and be loved. Can we also offer each other that freedom to have our different interests and friendships, freedom to be who we are, so that love can truly flower?

In love, we find that we can rest and feel safe in the presence of the beloved and truly be ourselves. When we know that we are loved we can take risks, knowing that we will not be cast out, that there will be someone to stand by us. In this kind of love we can heal and be healed.

Each new day is a chance to love deeply, to give thanks for the blessings in our lives and to live with gratitude and appreciation. Living in this way is a real key to contentment and happiness. It becomes clear that a thankful heart is a joyful one. And to bring joy to the one you love is a great gift. Joy is contagious and as we offer it out, it multiplies and grows.

It is also helpful to remember that we aren't just two isolated beings who have only each other to turn to. We are connected deeply to our tribe of family and friends and can turn to them for love and support as well.

So, as these two people embark on the incredible journey through this powerful portal of marriage, we wish them all the best. When we think or speak of them, let us remember the power of our thoughts and words. As their witnesses today we are called to be a support and an encouragement to them, to hold in our hearts their highest good. It is really something tangible we can do to support their lives together.

Probably the highest purpose of marriage is the embodiment of love, for love is the glue that holds the whole universe together. It is a force that inspires and ignites us. And although we can find it in another let us never forget that the source of love is within our own heart.

So let us rejoice today in the love between these two beautiful young people and let it be an inspiration in our own lives. There is always room for more loving.

That Lives in Us

If you put your hands on this oar with me
they will never harm another, and they will come to find
they hold everything you want.

If you put your hands on this oar with me, they would no
longer lift anything to your mouth
that might wound your precious land –
that sacred earth that is
your body.

If you put your soul against this oar with me,
the power that made the universe will enter your sinew
from a source not outside your limbs, but from a holy realm
that lives in us.

Exuberant is existence, time a husk.
When the moment cracks open, ecstasy leaps out and
devours space;
Love goes mad with the blessings, like my words give.

Why lay yourself on the torturer's rack of the past and the
future?
The mind that tries to shape tomorrow beyond its capacities
will find no rest.

Be kind to yourself dear – to our innocent follies.
Forget any sounds or touch you knew that did not help you
dance.
You will come to see that all evolves us.

If you put your heart against the earth with me, in serving
every creature, our Bleoved will enter you from our sacred
realm
and we will be, we will be
so happy. (65)

~Rumi (tr. Ladinsky)[ii]

Four Steps to Reconnect

This practice, inspired by Thich Nhat Hanh's ritual "Beginning
Anew" for resolving friction between community members in Plum

---

[ii] *Love Poems from God: Twelve Sacred Voices from the East and West* (New York: Penguin,
2002), p. 65. Copyright © 2002 by Daniel Ladinsky

Village France (Resource 7) is excellent for any relationship where difficulty and challenges or even just some small resistance or tension has crept in. Disruption is often the first step toward greater freedom and this practice has the potential to transform a *breakdown* in relating to a *breakthrough*.

I have used this as a practice for couples who aren't speaking to each other, and it has had positive and even some very tender and touching results.

To reconnect in this way is to look deeply and honestly at ourselves, our past actions and words so as to create a fresh start in our relationships with others. When a difficulty arises in our relationships and one of us feels resentment or hurt, it is a perfect time to do this practice. Begin by being clear in yourself what your hurt or issue is. If we are willing to courageously explore our own shadow through the reflections of another, much can be gained and potentially transformed.

Just one person speaks at a time and is not interrupted. The others practice deep listening and following their breath. (It can be helpful to have one or two others present whom you trust and respect to hold the space during this powerful but gentle process, especially if there is a lot of tension between the two participants.) You can use a bell between each of the four steps if it is useful to give everyone a chance to integrate and breathe. Here are the four steps:

1. *Appreciate*. Share what you each admire and value about the other person – this could be general qualities, or particular actions or words. This practice may support the other's personal development and lessen their suffering, as well as potentially opening and softening all our hearts by acknowledging these qualities.

2. *Apologise* for any suffering you may have caused or any regrets you may have.

3. *Articulate* any suffering or hurt you have experienced through the other person's words or deeds using "I" statements rather than blame.

4. *Ask* for support with our own suffering, from whatever cause. This can help others to better understand us and to know how they can offer assistance to help transform our suffering.

This practice offers a safe container to share our appreciation as well as our hurts or concerns, and Thây teaches that it "helps us develop our kind speech and compassionate listening". We all have strengths and weaknesses and this allows us to support and develop positive and useful qualities in ourselves and our relationships. As in a garden, when we water the seeds of loving kindness and compassion in each other, we also take energy away from the weeds of anger, jealousy, fear and misperception. This practice is not about trying to "fix" someone or some situation but about coming into right relationship with them and with ourselves.

We can practice this when needed or (even better) every day by expressing our appreciation for those around us, and apologizing right away when we do or say something that may have hurt them. The health and happiness of the whole community depends on the harmony, peace and joy that exist between each of its members. I hope you find this as useful and supportive for good relationships as we have.

Working with a Relationship Separation

No matter how well you do it, pain is inevitable in a separation, but it is possible to minimise the suffering for ourselves and those we have loved. We all make mistakes; this is part of learning. This realisation is humbling and can help us to forgive ourselves and others. Sometimes we may find ourselves wishing that we had done things differently, but what we can do is to make other, more conscious choices now. I remember despairing about the breakup of my first marriage. I felt guilt due to my Christian upbringing, and that I should make it work for our child and hang in there for her sake. We did try hard to make our breakup as harmonious as possible, but it is never as easy as one hopes it will be – so many hurt feelings, so many threads of one's life that are tied in together. Splitting up consciously and lovingly is a journey that can be filled with all kinds of emotions, some very desperate, but we can do our best. That is all we can ever do.

Below are some practices we have offered to couples who are separating, but have become stuck, and want support in moving on. If people you care about (or you yourself) are in this position, consider giving these practices a try. What is there to lose except your suffering?

As facilitator(s)/counsellor(s) we can ask the following question. How can we support you to move on with your lives; to be happy, to return to peace, to joy, and to let go of this suffering that has gone on for so long?

Can you, each of you, put yourselves in the skin of the other and feel the other person's suffering? The Tibetan art of *Tonglen* is a wonderful Buddhist practice we would like to offer you to do daily for a week, which is very transformative. It is a Buddhist version of walking a mile in my shoes. The practice is to find a quiet space and then to breathe in the challenges and suffering that you imagine that the other person is experiencing, and then to breathe out the balm of ease, lightness, even joy. See that person radiant, joyful, getting on with their lives. Free of suffering. Happy again. Do this for at least three minutes each day.

That is what we want for you both and yes, we know it is hard when there is anger and hurt feelings, but ultimately we know you want that peace for the other and for yourself. We can all get lost in the struggle at some points in our lives, but it is extremely stressful if we stay stuck there and don't find our way back to the stillness inside.

Would you be willing to do this practice for a week? (You can fake it till you make it.)

As we let go of the guilt and blame we can find a way through this. It is only really possible by being willing to "jump out of the system", meeting in the luminous field that we all long to live in and to act from. We are sometimes fearful and think we have to hold tight for things to work out, but the universe knows what we need and how to bring it about if we can just let go and let that miraculous energy of Spirit take the reins. Things can and do find their way.

There is one more practice that we would like to offer, usually also requesting that you do it daily for a week (minimum). It is a variation of Harry Palmer's "Compassion Exercise", which I have found helpful on my own journey. His practice involves trying to empathise with strangers in busy places, to develop global compassion. However, in this variation of the exercise, you seek a quiet place to build compassion for a former life partner.

So find a peaceful space, empty your mind, focus only on the other, and silently acknowledge these truths, one by one.

Step 1 With attention on the [other] person, repeat to yourself: "Just like me, this person is seeking some happiness for his/her life."

Step 2 With attention on the person, repeat to yourself: "Just like me, this person is trying to avoid suffering in his/her life."

Step 3 With attention on the person, repeat to yourself: "Just like me, this person has known sadness, loneliness and despair."

Step 4 With attention on the person, repeat to yourself: "Just like me, this person is seeking to fulfill his/her needs."

Step 5 With attention on the person, repeat to yourself: "Just like me, this person is learning about life." [iii]

If you are willing to do the work first, it is possible to really meet with compassion and understanding.

We are never more than one grateful thought away from peace of heart. (65)
~Brother David Steindl-Rast

Celebrate the Differences

Gender differences (whether attributed to DNA, hormones or nurture) are cause for both celebration and conflict (Gray 2). Yet research shows that these differences are often superficial (Marchetti).

Men are from Mars, Women are from Venus
~John Gray

Men are from Earth, Women are from Earth… Deal with it
~Sandra Marchetti[21]

Beginning in the later 1980's, Rainer and I have participated in men's and women's groups, and found them both energising and transformative. I realised that I carried a lot of "juice" (unresolved energy) around gender issues at that time that I needed to work with and transform.

[iii] Excerpted with the permission of the author. The Compassion Exercise is one of thirty exercises that can be found in *Resurfacing®: Techniques for Exploring Consciousness* by Harry Palmer. ReSurfacing® is a registered trademark of Star's Edge, Inc. The Compassion Cards can also be purchased: http: avatarbookstore.com/Books-Publications/the compassion-card.html.

Working with the archetypes helped immensely. I recommend psychiatrist Jean Bolen's book *Goddesses in Every Woman* if you would like to explore for yourself these "powerful inner patterns" exemplified by the Greek goddesses (1). In our women's gatherings we would spend a whole day focusing on each archetype – Artemis (wild wisdom), Aphrodite (lover/priestess), Athena (career woman/father's daughter), Demeter (mother), Persephone (daughter who transforms through her descent into the underworld), Hera (queen/wife), Hestia (depth, awareness of impermanence) and Hecate (crone/liberation) – reclaiming all these parts of our psyche with the recognition that we need all our parts to be whole and coherent. With the help of visualisations, dance etc. we practiced embodying their strengths and being aware of their shadows in our own lives, looking to understand which energies we might need more of and which we might need to focus less on. We found it a very interesting and useful exploration. This certainly helped with my own healing of the trampled feminine, and to instead move towards integrating what it means to be an empowered woman.

During those times I compiled a Medicine Wheel (a variation of a teaching tool used by many indigenous cultures, often divided (like mine) by spokes radiating towards the points of a compass). That helped me to have a deeper understanding of how these energies all worked together and how we could access them more (or less) fully in our own lives. My intention was to try to summarise in one illustration: the archetypes; the supposed effects of embodying too much or too little of each; what seasons, elements, astrological signs, tarot suits and animal totems each is associated with; their roles and purposes; what emotions they are accessed through; and the journey. You can find this tool in Resource 8.

Transforming the Masculine

Jungian psychologist Robert Moore is a guiding figure in masculine ideology. In 1990, he and mythologist Douglas Gillette co-authored

King, Warrior, Magician, Lover: Rediscovering the Archetypes of the Mature Masculine. Moore continues to inspire personal transformation through lectures and books such as *The Archetype of Initiation.* He believes that great change takes place in the presence of the divine (the "numinous"), and recommends the following process.

1. Realise the need for change.
2. Enter a sacred space with a shaman, priestess or skilled group leader.
3. Deal with that task that you have been avoiding.
4. Bring this transformation back into your life.

Whether working with the masculine or feminine energy, these four steps are appropriate. We all need to face parts of ourselves that we have been avoiding and make our inner demons conscious so that we can then use these energies to ignite rather than hinder our process of growth. It is all as Ram Dass likes to say "grist for the mill".

The Goddess Way

Whether male or female it is important to be in right relationship with ourselves. What follows is from an interview I gave for *Women's Spirituality Magazine* in 1995, with additional photographs (i.e. Fig. 3).

My "formal religious" background featured God as a transcendental being, a Father that one could petition favours from by being a "good girl". That's what was offered. But what really fed me spiritually was nature (the lapping of the waves below our cottage, the cries of the loons at twilight, lying in the long grass feeling the earth beneath me and the infinite vastness above), my grandmother's gentle quiet way of serving us children porridge in the morning, a touch of a loving hand or a smile, singing myself to sleep and dancing in the corridor. As I grew I realised that most of the outward religious representatives were males.

In later years it became important to find a new way. A way which honoured us as woman. Now one of my greatest joys is to watch and encourage women to reclaim their power (as well as reclaiming my own). For me this has been an essential step, bringing that Transcendental Male Sky God to Earth, no longer purely celestial or disconnected from me and from my body or the body of the planet. It is all that and more. That energy is juicy and alive. There is no duality in it, just one

Figure 3. Goddess of compassion, Kwan Yin (Tara), welcomes all to the Sanctuary at Mana Retreat Centre.

all-embracing field of energy that includes everything. There is earth and sky, joy and grief, exuberance and stillness, all waxing and waning. I am part of everything and everything is part of me. Spirituality is no longer about living in order to be eligible for a place in heaven but about living life wholeheartedly here and now.

The body I now see as a gateway (certainly not a hindrance), a doorway to the presence which vibrates within and all around.

Studying the ancient ways of the Goddess Path, and discovering a time when, cross-culturally, women were in their power and seen as sacred vessels of the divine feminine energy, has been very important for my own growth and understanding. So has creating ritual space with women where we can work together to reclaim that power which lives within us all. We air our wounds, encourage each other to be all that we are, and honour our bodies, our sexuality and our bleeding time. We are coming home to ourselves.

I would like to consciously express that Spirit in everything that I do:

- in the songs that I sing from my heart;
- in my dance as I let go and let the energy move me;
- in planting and growing the food that nourishes my family and caring for Mother Earth;
- in supporting and nourishing those around me and letting myself be nourished and supported by them;
- in my massage when I empty myself and share conscious touch with another in a way that nurtures and heals;
- in my sexuality as I open and share that sacredness with my partner;
- in trusting my inner guidance to show me the way, and the deep intuition in the belly; and
- in allowing myself to be all that I am and encouraging others to be their own unique selves.

I walk the Goddess Way in the beautiful hills where I live (Figure 4) and I know myself to be part of a wholeness. I see my purpose here on Earth as really being very simple: to love, serve and remember; to remember the truth of who I am and to awaken and live as consciously as I can in each moment. When I don't, I can forgive myself and return to that remembrance.

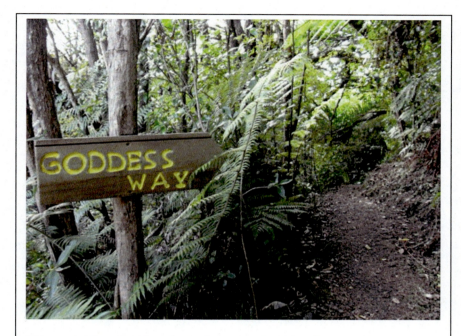

Figure 4. The Goddess Way forest trail, Mana Retreat Centre.

My spirituality is my life really; it is the force, the energy that moves me. It's how I start my day asking for guidance and trusting what unfolds. It is the way, it is life itself. I can't and don't want to separate anything from it. I honour all our emotions – the anger, the grief, the joy – as part of the energy flow which, like nature, needs to move through us. The trick is to not get stuck anywhere. The emptier we can be of a separate sense of self the more we can be filled with what is and in touch with our true nature.

My intention is to live and work in a way that has the possibility of transforming people (including myself), our culture and how we relate to each other and our planet. That is what I consider to be the political action I am engaged in. We need to start right where we are, in our homes, in our relationships, in our work, to begin to relate to life as a unity, an interconnected tapestry where each part makes a difference. If I can live my life in a way that reflects that wholeness, I am empowered and I choose to empower others so that our planet can truly begin to know peace. As long as women are hidden in the background, peace is not possible. We must rise together in strength and grace. Then true equality can begin to manifest. Not sameness, but real equality where woman and all that she stands for is recognised as immensely important. The planet needs the feminine energy to heal its wounds and come back into balance, and it is happening. Let us collectively infuse our world with love.

The rituals that we share in our women's group serve to connect us to the sacredness of our bodies and all of life, and to the goddess within in which "we live and move and have our being" (Bible, Acts 17:28). As we step into the depth of understanding of what that really means, we realise that "the Goddess is alive and magic is afoot!"[22]

Let us tend well the garden of our relationships, whether it be with ourselves or another. In the end what really matters is how much we have loved. If we take care and offer our best it is likely that we will be blessed with many delicious fruits. We can ask ourselves, "How tolerant am I able to be?" For as we journey together much is asked of each of us and our challenges will be many. If we extend tolerance and loving kindness to each other, it creates a generous heart and brings more joy and lightness into our lives, lessening and easing the suffering encountered along the way.

A delightful verse from the poem "How Does it Feel to be a Heart" is easy to memorise and be with:

For all I know is love,
And I find my heart Infinite
And Everywhere! (36)

~ Hafiz (tr. Ladinsky)[iv]

[iv] *I Heard God Laughing: Poems of Hope and Joy.* (New York: Penguin, 2006). Copyright © 2006 Daniel Ladinsky

CHAPTER FOUR: BUDDHIST PRINCIPLES

There is only one time when it is essential to awaken. That time is now.

~Buddha

In this chapter, I've gathered together some of the Buddhist principles that have been so helpful for me over the last 40 years, and can be useful guidelines no matter what path you are on. I have been blessed to study under a number of revered masters, and this is a chance to share and summarise some of these great teachings. The Buddha has said, yes, there is suffering *and* there is a way out of suffering, which he outlines clearly in the Eightfold Path.

Four Noble Truths

After his enlightenment, the Buddha's first teaching was a discourse on the Four Noble Truths, which formed the basis of Buddhism. There is suffering, and we need to understand it. This is the path that leads to liberation.

1.   *The truth of suffering* or *dukkha* (which needs to be acknowledged)

Death, decay and pain will afflict us all. Don't be ashamed to admit you suffer. Everyone suffers. Our willing acceptance of struggle in our lives is the first step on the path of awakening. Admitting the struggle is the spiritual path, not some unfortunate obstacle to it. We get in touch with our mind/body experience of feeling limited or tethered (a sense of imprisonment). We can then look deeply at the cause of our struggling.

2.   *The truth of the cause of suffering*
We need to understand that the main causes of suffering are desire (craving for what we don't have) and attachment or *tanha* to what we have.

Buddha saw that what binds us to this wheel of sorrow is in our own minds. Out of ignorance we become attached to these four desires. The first attachment is to craving for sense pleasures. The second attachment is to our own opinions and viewpoints, which keeps us from seeing things as they truly are. Reality is then filtered through our own small coloured window.

> *If you wish to know the truth… only cease to cherish*
> *opinions.*
>
> ~ Seng-Ts'an, Third Zen Patriarch

The third attachment is to particular rites and rituals and ways of doing things, thinking that our way is the right way. The fourth attachment Buddha speaks of is to a belief in self, in an "I". Our attachment to this belief is so strong that our life usually revolves around it. If we could let this go, we would loosen the cords that bind us so tightly.

Ignorance regarding the true nature of desire/craving is said to be the root cause of the problem. Out of this ignorance we become attached.

> *When… the impulse to grasp at desires is restrained, then*
> *desire no longer appears as the demon responsible for our*
> *unhappiness… Learn how to live with desire without*
> *being stung by it.*
>
> ~ Ajahn Munindo

The cause of suffering is simply the desire for anything other than what is.

3.   *The truth of the end of suffering* (which needs to be experienced and realised)

There is no higher happiness than peace. ~ The Buddha

To end suffering, lay down the burden of the self-cherishing "I". *Most misery comes from being self-focused,* as our illusion of separateness is what binds us to our suffering. There is no one to blame for our suffering. *Nirvana* is a state which opens all our doors so that freedom and peace can appear. Our greatest challenges, if we face them, can be our gateway. In that way, our struggles can propel us towards awakening.

4.   *The truth of the way out of suffering* (this needs to be lived)
The way to this state of profound peace is the Noble Eightfold Path, which must be walked by each of us, teaching us how to lay down the burden. Let us explore that well-laid-out path of awakening step by step.

Noble Eightfold Path

1.   *Right understanding* (right view)
We must understand certain laws such as karma (cause and effect). Every action brings a certain result and has consequences. Whenever we act motivated by greed, hatred or delusion, then pain and suffering come back to us. When our actions are motivated by generosity, love or wisdom, the results are happiness and peace. We must also understand the importance of:

- generosity as an expression of non-attachment,
- letting go, and

- the special relationships we have with our parents along with the requisite responsibilities. The Buddha advised in the *Pali Canon* that even if we carried our parents on our backs for the rest of our lives we would never repay them for this precious gift of a human rebirth.

Right understanding also involves knowing our true nature, and the nature of impermanence, developed through meditation. When we know that "this too shall pass", that everything changes, it can help us to let go and to loosen our grip on needing things or people to be a certain way. Finally, we must understand that there is no separate self: all is interbeing.

Suffering is resistance to what is.[23]

* * *

Suffering arises from trying to make permanent that which is impermanent.

* * *

It is our very search for perfection outside of ourselves that causes our suffering. It is not perfection we must seek, but freedom of the heart.

* * *

We do not exist as separate beings.

~ The Buddha

Mahamudra (which means "great vehicle" in the Mahayana path of Buddhism) points us towards the direct seeing of our true nature. The Buddha advises us to cultivate that and to be like a hollow bamboo, empty, just allowing things to be as they are.

2.   *Right thought*
Our thoughts are powerful; they inform our words and actions. Right thought involves right intention; our perceptions condition our actions. Right thought is free of judgement, grasping, aversion, and ill will. Freedom from ill will is freedom from anger – being able to

recognise anger as it arises and let it go. Right thought is free of negativity, opening instead to compassion and loving kindness. We must understand that thoughts are impermanent and are seeds that can be constructive or destructive or let go of altogether. We can experiment with not making assumptions about people or situations, which we subsequently believe to be true. We can then ask for clarification instead of creating a whole big drama in our minds.

The next three steps involve how we relate to others and cultivating skilful means (our outer life).

3. Right speech
Right speech means being aware of the suffering caused by telling lies (or even exaggerating), gossiping, slandering, blaming, complaining, or using abusive or harsh language. Speak that which is honest, wholesome, skilful and helpful, creating peace and harmony, and using loving and kind speech. Speak that which unites rather than separates, saying what we need to say but skilfully and with wisdom. We can explore moving towards being more mindful with our speech, while practicing deep listening in order to bring happiness to others and to ease suffering.

4. Right action
Right action means being aware of the suffering caused by hurting others, doing our best not to intentionally harm, kill or steal (taking that which isn't given), and not engaging in sexual activities that we know will cause pain to others.

5. Right livelihood
Right livelihood means engaging in work which is helpful and supportive to others, which does not involve intentionally hurting, stealing or dishonesty. It is important to like what we do and to bring our best to it; to do what we do in a sacred manner, with awareness.

The next three have to do with our meditation (inner work).

6. Right effort
Find a way to make efforts to reduce suffering without forcing. No-one is going to do it for you. In *Being Peace*, Thich Nhat Hanh uses

this analogy: when we're lost, we can head towards a guiding star (88). It doesn't mean we'll ever get there, but we can do our best to go in that direction. The more we are able to see and acknowledge our particular patterns of resistance, the more they will begin to loosen their grip on us.

In *Living Buddhist Masters*, Kornfield cites Ramana Maharshi (1879-1950):

> *No one succeeds without effort. Mind control is not your birthright. Those who succeed owe their liberation [or success] to their perseverance.* (9)

7. *Right mindfulness*

Right mindfulness means being aware of what is happening in the present moment, calling the mind home again and again, remembering to be present for any element of struggle in this moment and seeing into its causes. Mindfulness brings the qualities of poise, equilibrium and balance to the mind. We can breathe and choose to soften. There is no escape from the mind; the only way to be at peace is to be at ease with all that arises.

8. *Right concentration*

Right concentration is one pointedness of mind: the ability of the mind to stay steady on the object on which it is focused. This is meditation, to keep arriving right here into this moment.

The path is not about giving up the good things in our life but to wisely release the causes of suffering, discerning for ourselves what supports awakening and what obscures it. The Buddha advises us never to do anything just because he says so. Find out for yourself.

The Six Perfections (*Paramitas*) – *The Path of the Bodhisattva*

The six Great Friends (Perfections) will support your practice and your life to flourish. They are:[24]

1. *Dāna* – generosity;
2. *Sila* – wholesome relationships, conscious living, not causing harm intentionally;
3. *Ksãnti* – patience;
4. *Virya* – energy/effort/enthusiasm/enthusiastic perseverance;
5. *Samādhi or dyhana* – concentration (centredness, insight, clarity), focus; and
6. *Prajñã* – wisdom.

The first four need to be in place before meditation can really happen. Again they all link together. Generosity helps us have wholesome relationships, which is right living, which brings about patience. Then energy and enthusiasm are naturally there (and not drained away). This allows us to concentrate and focus and then wisdom/insight flowers. Once we have worked with these they spiral around again ("the transcendental six perfections") and we can work with them all again on a much deeper level.

*If we are having trouble with our relationships and feel they are difficult, back-track – work with generosity first and things will shift. When we find we can't be centred in meditation it is often because the other *paramitas* need attending to. If we practice dwelling in the radiance of loving kindness along with these qualities we will soon understand why they are called the six great friends.

Taking Refuge

Taking refuge is a cornerstone to Buddhist practice, but no matter what path you are following (or not) this practice of "Taking Refuge" in "Universal form" that Tarchin Hearn shares in his *Daily Puja* can be a very beneficial start to your day.

I take refuge in Wisdom
I take refuge in Compassion
I take refuge in Non-clinging Awareness

May I develop the six perfections
And awaken speedily for the sake of all living beings. (6)

More traditionally, one takes refuge in the Triple Gem: the Buddha (including one's own Buddha nature), the *Dharma* (the teachings which show us the way) and the *Sangha* (spiritual companions who support our journey and help us to stay on the path of awakening). Traditional wisdom and spiritual community are important in all paths, but in Buddhism they are recognised as a major priority.

The Four Divine Abidings (The Brahma *Vihāras*)

The Qualities
The potential is to abide in these four radiant states. Cultivating them by consciously practicing them brings untold benefits to our inner and outer lives.

- Loving kindness for all beings = *Metta;*
- The love and compassion that transforms suffering = *Karuna;*
- Sympathetic joy, the immense joy one feels for others' good fortune = *Mudita;*
- The love that is non attached, content, balanced (calm abiding), equanimity = *Upekkha.*

Near Enemies (to be aware of and to watch out for in ourselves):
- of loving kindness are attachment (clinging, fear, controlling);
- of compassion would be pity;
- of sympathetic joy are judgement and comparison; and
- of equanimity would be indifference.

Shadows (important to stay alert when we notice any of these arising in ourselves):
- of loving kindness are manipulating, controlling and

bargaining;

- of compassion are burnout, depression, a need to fix or rescue others;
- of sympathetic joy are manic elation, not seeing the suffering of others; and
- of equanimity are apathy, or just doing nothing.

Four Practices to Deal with Negative Seeds

(Here are a few practices which can support us to work with these challenging energies when they arise)

1. If they are sleeping, just leave them alone. Don't water your seeds of anger, despair, etc.
2. If a negative seed manifests (like anger), then practice so that this mental formation can return to the store consciousness. And do what needs to be done: for example if hate music is playing, change the CD.
3. Water any positive seeds, such as joy, understanding, generosity and love... Do a retreat, read a *dharma* book, sing, or walk in nature.
4. Once these positive seeds have manifested, encourage them to stay by continuing to nourish and water them. The following awarenesses and practices can help to water these skilful seeds.

Keys to Awakening *Samata*
(Harmony/Balance/Equanimity)

Four keys to help awaken these qualities in our lives are to:

1. smile;
2. breathe, relax, be at ease;
3. be present; and
4. appreciate (the awesome wonders of life). Notice the beauty all around.

Make a decision to let go of clinging to separation and suffering.

Walking Meditation

Mindful walking can be done almost anywhere, but nature is especially conducive. As our steps slow down so can our minds. We can enjoy walking peaceful steps upon the Earth. Here are a few points that can support the practice:

1. Be aware of heart fullness; walk feeling your body moving through space (let this be global).
2. Be aware of the breath and explore whether it can find a connection to your walking (e.g. breathing in four steps, breathing out four steps). Don't force a connection, just observe.
3. Be aware that you are walking on a living being (Mother Earth).
4. Smile softly, inwardly.

The Five Hindrances

(When we understand how these are linked we have the possibility of transforming this cycle so it doesn't have to keep repeating in our lives. I invite you to explore this for yourself, perhaps noticing the places you tend to get stuck.)

1. Desire (wanting more than what is in the flow of the moment; resistance to what is – a recipe for suffering)
   One who verbalises a lot is usually stuck here. This can lead to...

2. Ill will (feeling anger/frustration and usually projecting and blaming someone else such as a partner or authority figure – aversion may follow)
   This then leads (due to leakage of energy) to...

3. Sloth and torpor (draining energy, resulting in dullness of body and mind, and exhaustion)
   After lethargy, laziness, no energy, then comes...

4. Restlessness of body and mind (with worry/anxiety one is agitated, unable to focus)
    Leading to…

5. Sceptical doubt, depression, hopelessness (unable to function properly)
    One can get stuck here for a long time until the cycle begins again unless we become alert and willing to make different choices.

Working with these hindrances (impermanent mental factors)
Recognise (name) them – recognition leads to mindfulness. This hindrance is not "I", this is a mental factor and it will pass. If it doesn't pass, work with it. Make friends with it, face it – find what is behind it. Ask, "What is needed here?"

Pillars of Dharma (Activity that Supports Awakening)

1. *Generosity.* Giving becomes the cause of great happiness in our lives. When we have this revelation our life begins to really flower. The karmic results of generosity are abundance and deep harmonic relationships with other people. Through practice we can develop spontaneous generosity.

2. *Moral restraint* means to do our best to cultivate and practice the five basic precepts.

3. *Meditation.* There are two streams –
    a. *Samata* (development of concentration, calm abiding/ bliss); and
    b. *Vipassana* (insight, experiencing the flow of impermanence, wisdom, no separate self).

*The insight into impermanence is the beginning of all freedom. According to Thich Nhat Hanh:

> *Some people say that Buddhist practice is to dissolve the self. They do not understand that there is no self to be dissolved. There is only the notion of self to be transcended.*

111

The Four Efforts (or Exertions)

Important steps to awakening.
The key is to make these efforts as soon as these states arise.
1. Make an effort to become aware of the presence of an unwholesome state, such as anger or depression. Investigate what caused it to arise.
2. Take steps to let it go. Choose not to create the conditions that will make it arise in the future.
3. Recognise any wholesome state that is present, such as joy, compassion or generosity.
4. Take steps to extend this wholesome state: support any conditions that encourage it.

When an unwholesome state arises, recognise it – this is an opportunity to come back to a wholesome state…Three breaths is sometimes all it takes.

Four Gates to Awakening (Illumination)

Wise effort is important, but in the end the awakening heart comes as an act of grace. We can enter through any one of these four gates:

1. The gate of sorrow – life on earth is painful as well as beautiful, opening our hearts wide to the suffering of the world (compassion);
2. The gate of emptiness – selflessness and the emptiness of all phenomena; the dissolving of the self-cherishing "I";
3. The gate of oneness (*Satori*) – experiencing and recognising the interconnectedness of all of life – interbeing;
4. The gate of the eternal present – where we are going is here and now (the gateless gate). Mindfulness.

Which of these gates resonates the most with your journey?

Buddha, when asked about the path of practice, said that there *are four ways spiritual life unfolds:*

1. quickly and with pleasure (opening and letting go easily);
2. quickly but painfully (a death, loss etc);
3. gradually and accompanied with pleasure; and
4. slowly and gradually – often through suffering.

There is an old Zen saying,

> *Before enlightenment, chop wood, carry water.*
> *After enlightenment, chop wood, carry water.*[25]

The difference is the attitude and awareness that we bring to the task at hand, because although living in a body always requires doing, we can bring our being into our doing.

Map of Awakening

The Buddha spoke of four progressive stages of awakening:

1. Entering the stream – our first taste of absolute freedom. We see the illusion of the separate self and begin to awaken to a sense of timeless peace.
2. Returning again – purification. We discover and release the coarsest habits of grasping and aversion that keep us bound to a limited sense of self. We see the suffering that arises when we cling to our desires and fears. Finally – often in deep meditation – the strongest of these forces falls away.
3. Non-returning – We are released from any remaining desire, grasping, anger and fear. Clinging is abandoned the moment it arises. The heart's deep peace is rarely disturbed.
4. Great awakening – the last traces of subtle clinging (even to freedom and joy) fall away. The radiance of our true nature shines unhindered. Be a light unto yourself.

Everything is mind-made.

* * *

Those who grasp after views and opinions only wander
about the world annoying people.

~ The Buddha

Seng Ts'an says that enlightenment dawns only when we are "without anxiety about non-perfection". We meet the world with our heart as it is, unafraid of its beauty or its blemishes. Ordinary perfection is being true to ourselves, to the way things are. Our spiritual task is not to try to be perfect but to awaken to the perfection of all that is around us. Shunryu Suzuki Roshi wrote:

When we realize the everlasting truth of "everything
changes" and find our composure in it, we find ourselves in
Nirvana. (91)

What Really Matters?

There are so many things in life that appear to be important, but what really matters? The Buddha speaks of wisdom, compassion, and purity. I must add loving kindness.

Wisdom – functions by seeing through the way things appear to be to the way things actually are (insight). An example of wisdom would be to understand the truth of impermanence: that all conditioned phenomena are impermanent. Right understanding of interbeing – understanding that there is no separate self – is also wisdom.

Compassion – means "feeling with" life. Compassion is a sense of empathetic relationship in the context of suffering, opening to the pain of others and ourselves with no judgement, no barrier. Don't explain the pain away, just hold it and receive it without being overwhelmed by it. It may have something important to tell us. Whenever we ourselves suffer, it is an opportunity to learn compassion. Great compassion (*Maha Karuna*) is unconditional love which requires lots of good heartedness.

Purity – is the absence of "this is my wisdom or my compassion". Selfishness or self focus is devoid of this purity, whereas a broader view allows us to see that all life is connected and interdependent; every being is seeing things from their own viewpoint. What you see is a reflection of you. A free being shows great interest in all the aspects of life, but is not bound by any of them; in the world but not of the world.

Wisdom understands whereas compassion feels, holds and receives the situation.

> *… The busier our minds are, the less we feel the heart's natural impulse to awaken.*
>
> ~ Ajahn Munindo

When we sit in alignment, anchored in the heart, the layers and obstructions will reveal themselves. Stay with it, go deeper, welcome it all into the field. In his insight meditation retreats ("The Heart of Understanding"), Jeremy Logan teaches that cultivation of awareness (mindfulness) is to "bring a [quality of] non-judgmental attention to our lives" when sitting, walking, breathing, listening, and talking.

Dealing with Anger or Sadness

> *Breathing in, I calm the activities of the mind in me.*
>
> * * *
>
> *Breathing in, I recognize my feeling.*
> *Breathing out, I calm my feeling.*[26]
>
> ~ The Buddha

In a discourse I attended in 2005, Thich Nhat Hanh said that, "When I am angry I go back to my breathing. In that time I don't speak or act (I just breathe). I know that anger has arisen and I need to take care of it". When anger (or sadness) arises we can:

1. Recognise our anger, neither feeding it nor denying it.
2. Learn how to care for it. Breathing in, be aware that anger has arisen. Breathing out, "I am here for you".
3. Bring mindfulness to our anger to be in right relationship with it, not possessed by it. The wisest way is to see it and tend to it (not suppress it but allow it to be). Mindfulness is the energy that takes care of the anger. This is a dangerous time to speak or act as it could be very destructive or hurtful to the other person.

The Buddha advises that holding on to anger is like drinking poison. (At a retreat I did with Adyashanti in 2007, he pointed out that your body is your barometer as to when things are out of harmony. Listen to it. Your thoughts immediately become embodied. For example, if you think you don't like a person, your jaw may clench.)

Remember, it is nothing special to just seek your own happiness – but to seek happiness for all beings, that is special and brings tremendous joy.

> *The wave needs to know it is not just a wave, but it is the whole ocean.*
>
> * * *
>
> *Let's help each other let go of the fictitious self.*
>
> * * *
>
> *Boredom only happens when we are not actively engaged with life.*
>
> ~ Adyashanti, at a retreat in 2007

It has been said that the butter is in the milk, but unless you churn the milk you don't get the butter. Similarly, Buddha nature is within us but unless we practice (cultivate) it, we will not experience it.[27]

When you realize how perfect everything is,
You will tilt your head back and laugh at the sky.[28]

Signs of Awakening

Waking up brings more freedom, joy and lightness into our lives. We may notice more of the following seeping into our way of being in the world:

- laughter;
- calmness, stillness;
- spontaneous joy and serenity (bliss);
- a sense of connectedness with all of life, interbeing;
- slowing down of the monkey mind;
- taking things as they come (resistance dissolves);
- breathing becoming more natural, more relaxed; and
- experiencing a greater sense of clarity, spaciousness and wisdom.

At the retreat I attended in 2007, Adyashanti explained that being awake means knowing that your individual separate sense of self has no independent existence. As the wave is the ocean, you are existence. You are nothing and everything.

Don't try to know your true self through the mind. The mind is your tool but not your true self. Mind is deceptive. Truth is unchanging; mind is always changing. The mind like a cloud can obscure the sky, but the inner being like the sky space is always free. The day will come when you know that only awareness exists, that spacious awareness is the true self. Don't cling to the mind fragments (your filters), but instead focus on the space. That space, like the sky, is clear and forever free. Put your attention on the space that you are. Can you take a moment right now to pause, breathe and sense into that spaciousness?

The deeper you journey with yourself the quieter you become. When the mind is still and there is only that sense of being, that is your true self. These states of mind may be encountered as you explore these inner terrains.

Three Minds

1. *Big mind* – expansive, all inclusive, senses interbeing with all of life.
2. *Caring mind* – (parental mind) – empathy and compassion arising.
3. *Joyous mind / letting go mind* – knows the joy of releasing (rather than accumulating), takes things as they come with joy and gratitude and then lets go.

If you are doing this work you usually find yourself in the lab – curious, enquiring, looking deeply into other dimensions, exploring and discovering the inner and outer realms… or as a *bodhisattva* out in the world caring for others, looking after the wounded, doing what needs to be done.

> *The heart has the capacity to love everyone.*
> *This is an aspect of Buddha-Nature.*
> *Cultivate Buddha nature.*
> *Love everyone.*[29]

This lovely verse comes to us as a gift from Thich Nhat Hanh:

> *Waking up this morning, I smile.*
> *Twenty-four brand-new hours are before me.*
> *I vow to live fully each moment*
> *And to look at all beings with eyes of compassion.* (19)

CHAPTER FIVE: THE HEALING POWER OF SOUND

I am passionate about singing. Most of us have experienced that music has the power to speak directly to the heart. I rejoice in this direct communion often experienced while singing or sounding. My mother told me that I sang before I could talk, and singing has been a major form of nourishment and creative expression ever since. Even as a teenager, on the bus to school I would be singing my heart out to the pop tunes of the 60's. Much later in 1992, simultaneously to our choir starting, I began an intense and fascinating journey with the Lichtenberg Institute in Germany that evolved into doing a training with them, then called "Healing Through Sound". Now in 2016 I am still on that journey, astounded by the powerful effect of sound on the body, mind and spirit. I hope you find this chapter interesting and perhaps even helpful for your own sound explorations.

It is time for us to realise individually and collectively the deep impact that sound has and to be able to use this to move to subtler levels of our being. Hazrat Inayat Khan, a Sufi mystic and musician, refers to music as the language of the soul. He says that "music is the best medium" for awakening the soul (76).[30]

This music, this vibration, which is the very source of all matter, was often known to the ancient mystics as the music of the spheres. It can be heard by those who have begun to listen deeply, those who know the art of silence and meditation.

Everyone knows how music can stir the emotions, uplift the spirit and open the heart, whether making music or just listening to it. I am sure we have all recognised it as a potential gateway to something greater and vaster than our ordinary sense of self. There are moments when suddenly there is just sound pulsing through. Profound experiences of oneness can occur where our self-imposed boundaries dissolve and then we can get a glimpse of our interconnectedness with all of life.

In this chapter we will explore what makes sound healing and look at simple techniques we can do ourselves or share with others that will help us access this powerful tool on our journey to awakening consciousness.

It is intriguing to note that the changes going on in the high frequencies occurring in the human voice are also happening to the Earth. The Earth also pulses at a particular vibration, which is around 8 Hertz ("Hz", vibrations per second). This has been rising rapidly towards 13 Hz. (Interesting to note that 13,000 Hz is now arising in the voice.) This all ties into the golden mean which I shall discuss later. Gregg Braden has spoken of this in his book *Awakening to Zero Point*. He describes how we are moving together with our planet towards a higher state of consciousness, this higher level of frequency and vibration. "All life within the envelope of Earth's vibratory influence attempts to 'match' their frequencies to that of the Earth. To this end, each cell of your body is constantly shifting patterns of energy to achieve harmonic resonance to the reference signals of our planet" (30). Always the molecule with the lower frequency will have a tendency to try to match (through resonance) the higher frequency, as with a tuning fork. Each cell of our body tries to match the Earth's rhythmic pulse or heartbeat. "As our physical bodies attempt to maintain this attunement, those areas holding inharmonic energies of trauma (psychological, emotional or physical) begin to vibrate out of sync, dislodging the energies of emotions that no longer fit". This often occurs in the sound work and when people begin to receive these high frequencies (either through singing themselves or being sung into). Then a lot of trauma can begin to be released from the body. Twitches or jerks can be triggered in any area of the body and are no cause for alarm. I have experienced this myself. This is simply the body releasing stored trauma and it is best to relax and let it go.

Hazrat Inayat Khan in his book *The Music of Life* states that "the belief held by the ancients was that the creative Source in its first step towards manifestation was audible and in its next step visible". Every form that we see in this objective world has been constructed by sound and is sound. Swami Shyam had a deep impact on my understanding of sound and the source of sound. He often said that at the Absolute level there is no question of sound or colour. It is a pure, waveless state: the formless, unmanifest, Pure Void. Out of this comes sound. When this sound is struck there is a resonance which we refer to with the symbol *Om. Om* represents the vibration of this *Shabd-Brahm* (absolute sound field). This pure sound as it begins to crystallise produces light. This absolute sound field is the source of all thought, speech, action and form because forms are nothing but vibrations.

I would like to offer some techniques and ideas for working with the healing aspect of sound.

1. *Sound Current Meditation:* (1977, from Swami Shyam in Kullu, India at the International Meditation Institute). With your full attention listen to the centre of your head, the base of the brain, often referred to as the seat of consciousness. Listen to the highest pitch; do not get pulled into the ears or the outer sounds. Once you have begun to hear this high pitched cricket-like sound, expand out to include your whole body, then the space that you are in and then continue to expand your awareness to include the whole universe. This vibration is the *Om*. It is perceived directly by the brain and subtle bodies (non-physical attributes connected to the physical by energy points or *chakras*), not the organ of the ear. This directs the individual consciousness back to its source.

2. *Suma:* This is a Sufi practice for listening to music. Listen with your whole being, allowing yourself to be a medium of resonance for the music. This can move one to deep states of ecstasy.

3. *Note Sustaining:* Hazrat Inayat Khan says that for the mystical to be revealed the voice needs to come direct from the soul; that to sustain a note for a long time allows this to happen.[31] A resonance can occur which is like an echo of the vastness of the soul. The sound is directly connected to the feeling depth of the singer, who can momentarily tap into this divine energy.

4. *Free Flow:* Start toning, perhaps on a single vowel like a soft "o" or "ah" or even the sound of *"Om"* by yourself or in a group; have no agenda or idea of where you are going and be willing to risk, to move into the unknown. As you are toning, trust, stay just with the sound and see where it takes you. You will find it has a natural ebb and flow of its own. Sometimes it will be strong, sometimes you might find it getting very soft and tender. Listen to the sound as if you are watching the sun set. Allow it to happen through you. You can also try using a phrase or a few words like a prayer. For example it could be just a simple "Alleluiah" or a "Gloria" or even *"Kyrie Eleison"* or *"Om mane padme hum"*, *"Om Tare Tutarre Ture Soha"* or an English one like "Lord, make me an instrument of Thy peace". Let the words, the rhythm, the pitch find their own way. There are no rules except to listen and stay connected to your inner centre and to the whole group. This can be an amazing experience of unity. In the Kings' Chamber of the great pyramid in Egypt, in 1997, I experienced such a high voltage of energy moving in and through the sound, that I and those with me were transported to a realm of depth and power beyond words. Later, in a temple to Isis in Philae, I again experienced the sound linking me and the whole group to a very high energy space. In the state of consciousness that was invoked, we were able to move beyond time and space and tap into another dimension of reality. Again the energy that poured through the body vehicle was incredibly activating and energising.

5. *Methods from the Lichtenberg Institute:* The techniques we have studied are far too numerous to name but I will include a few simple exercises often called "stimuli". For example, all the senses can be used as doorways to being profoundly in the present moment and to open the spaces in our sound. Here is an exercise using smell as a gateway. You can work with essential oils (perhaps lavender, rose or cedar but almost any will do). First mindfully take a deep whiff of one of the oils, and then with that same feeling of openness (molecular spaciousness), sing just one tone, sustaining it for a long time, being totally with it. There is no forcing or efforting, just opening to the experience as it is.

6. *Inner Flying:* We have many different rhythms in our bodies, including: our heartbeat, breathing, and cranial sacral rhythm (to name just a few). It is possible to tune into your cranial sacral rhythm (for example, in your tongue) while singing. This can give a sense of inner flying that is extremely delightful. You can then allow this rhythm to enter into the sound, which responds, opening the sound to a place of freedom where the natural vibrato begins to come through.

7. *Deep Sounding:* In Lichtenberg we were taught that this can relax the larynx and allow it to drop slightly into a condition which helps to create brilliances in the voice. Begin by deeply relaxing (sitting up or lying down). Start making very deep, low sounds as you might imagine Tibetan monks producing. Any side noises like rattling or buzzing are all helpful to the process. Do this for as long as you feel to, and then make a tone at your normal pitch and notice the changes in your sound. It is important not to try to recreate the characteristics of the deeper sound, but to just trust that you got the information and the adjustments will be made. Relax and enjoy.

Except where I indicate another source, the information that follows is mainly from my notes taken during training sessions in the Lichtenberg method, with deep gratitude for all I have received.

It is interesting that although these healing frequencies cannot be forced, still there are certain conditions that can help open the way, such as an isometric state of calm alertness in which you are deeply relaxed in a meditative state and yet very present. This condition also creates a sense of connectedness with all of life. Put all thoughts aside, just be right here. Whatever arises, do not push it away but just allow it to be transformed by and through the sound. Be willing to move into the unknown without crutches and old patterns. This is extremely liberating.

Leonardo Fibonacci was a thirteenth century mathematician who discovered a sequence of numbers (0, 1, 1, 2, 3, 5, 8, 13, 21 and so on) with a ratio of 1 to 1.618, the golden ratio (or mean), one of the most important concepts in sacred geometry and physics. The Fibonacci spiral is a growth (logarithmic) spiral created using the golden ratio (Figure 5), and it occurs everywhere in nature, whether it be in a fern, a snail or our inner ear.[32] The design of the human body includes several other examples of the golden ratio (Figure 6).[33] These perfect proportions are delightful to the eye as well as the ear.

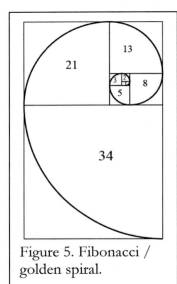

Figure 5. Fibonacci / golden spiral.

Singer formants, the frequencies at which a singer's voice can even be heard over an orchestra (3,000, 5,000, 8,000 and 13,000 Hz), are in a Fibonacci sequence that approximates these golden ratio proportions.[34] In fact it has been found that these sounds are incredibly healing for all of life, certainly for the human being as well as plants, animals and the Earth herself. The normal range of the human voice (the fundamental pitch) only reaches 1,500 Hz. These high frequencies, however, are transformative to hear and sing. All the senses are affected and awakened. The seeing becomes more light infused, colours more brilliant. Our sense of smell opens to deeper levels of receptivity, and hearing becomes very perceptive and refined. Our feeling sense becomes highly sensitive, finely tuned to deep levels of energy. Not only are the senses opened, cleansed and activated, they are also used as gateways to this healing sound. As we allow ourselves to open to these particular high frequencies in the human voice (which are also referred to as brilliances) our whole system is charged and energised. Ultimately we can merge with the source of all sound.

These high frequencies are also occurring all around us in nature. The sound of bees humming and some bird songs register at 3,000 Hz on a frequency analyser, a queen bee or cicada at 5,000 Hz, and a grasshopper at 8,000 Hz. These same frequencies occur in our bodies: 3,000 Hz in the external ear, 5,000 in the middle ear and 8,000 Hz in the brain stem. As we begin to hear these sounds internally and externally it awakens our ability to sing them. This is the music of the spheres, the very song of the cosmos within and without. I would like to encourage you to really

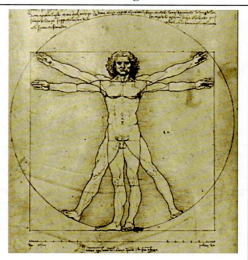

Figure 6. Leonardo da Vinci's drawing "Canon of Proportions" (1490). The proportions of the circle and square outlining the body are nearly a golden division. The navel is at a golden ratio point between hairline and foot.

listen to these inner sounds; they are always there – we just need to listen. As soon as we put our attention on them, there they are. Tuning in to them can be very calming, uplifting and meditative. I invite you to pause here, close your eyes, relax while taking a few conscious breaths and simply listen to these inner sounds; they are always present, but we need to become aware of them if we want to hear them. For me, it is like coming home.

Not all high frequencies are healing; for example, the shrill sound of a baby crying is around 4,000 Hz and is actually very painful to the ears. There is also a condition of the inner ear called tinnitus. People who suffer from tinnitus hear unpleasant sounds in their inner ear which are experienced as very disharmonious. They can be shrill or they can be low annoying sounds, very disturbing for those with this condition. We have a good friend and sound teacher/healer, Ruth Weimer, who practices at the Lichtenberg Institute in Germany. She works with bringing these sounds back into a harmonious balance so that clients are able to once again enjoy their inner sounds, which can be brought back in tune with the perfect proportions of the golden mean.

One of the prerequisites for brilliances to occur in the voice is a relaxing of the larynx, which then lowers slightly, causing the human body to move into these perfect proportions of the golden mean. Then the brilliances (singer formants) begin to appear in the voice. This code (the golden mean) is fundamental to life on our planet so it is not surprising to find that it also governs the fundamental vibration of the Earth itself. It is as if we and our planet are preparing to move to a higher vibrational level. We are awakening to the next step of our evolution together. A leap is required which requires willingness and trust.

A well known theory from quantum physics presents itself in this context: the chaos theory. It suggests that on the journey towards opening to these brilliances, the person singing needs to be willing to enter into chaos so that the energy to be freed can move into a higher order. This cannot be forced, only allowed. Like the boiling of water – as the heat is applied the molecules move into chaos until the moment that they reach boiling point. Then all the molecules leap into a synergetic higher order and begin to move together in the same way. One molecule starts and all the others rapidly follow (the hundredth monkey principle – after a certain critical point, the energy/idea spreads rapidly). This higher order needs less effort and works on its own. For this to happen in our sound we must first surrender our need to control and to have things a certain way. We then become vessels – channels – for the divine sound to pour through. These sounds carry a quality of emptiness and spaciousness that can only be described as the voice of the soul.

As our body moves into these perfect proportions (with the lowering of the larynx) our sound itself resembles a sacred space. It is highly resonant and charged with energy.

It is interesting to note that these are the same sounds (high frequencies) that are heard within in deep meditation. They have been measured with frequency analysers. The Hindus called these sounds *Om* and the Sufis *Hu* (the breath of the Eternal). No wonder they are so transformative. They produce a charging (loading) affect on the brain, bringing wakefulness, vitality and creativity, and uplifting one to a higher state of consciousness. As these higher frequencies start coming through they cleanse and energise the whole system. Sometimes the body literally vibrates (shakes) with the highly charged energy that is moving through it.

Most people are not aware of the differences between overtones and brilliance. The overtone is a higher frequency sound splitting off from the fundamental pitch; it is tied to the latter and has no freedom of its own. Brilliances are, however, bundles of high frequencies that appear out of the voice in response to certain stimuli. They later are integrated into the sound. Overtones are done with pressure; brilliance is effortless and requires no pressure. We can learn to access these particular frequencies to be used for healing and raising consciousness as well as increasing the velocity and radiant resonance of the voice. These sounds are akin to our very essence – they are the nectar (*Amrita*) of the gods. Once these frequencies begin to enter our sound it grows and we literally raise our vibrational level. The sound is coming through us as an autonomic function and takes on a very exulting quality. To be able to consciously create these healing sounds opens a multidimensional gateway that can have a profound effect on our inner journey.

There are three important parameters that help to bring the brilliance into being. These are vibrato (not a warble or a forced vibrato but the natural rhythm of the voice, which creates a spacious, molecular light-filled quality to the sound), vowel and pitch. We work with particular vowel sounds that enable the resonant quality of the brilliance to come through. With the pitch we begin by making tones mainly around two or three notes that are our most comfortable. This will be unique to each individual and of course varies between men and women. Men can work to bring in the lightness of the head (female) voice into their sound whereas women can bring in the depth and darkness of the chest voice into theirs. When we bring in these parameters and permit them to interact with each other and be affected by the brilliance, something very freeing begins to happen. A feedback loop is created, the inner intelligence seems to respond to that information, and the voice is transformed. All this creates a sort of zero point (the opposite of the hyper-pressure that most singers use), more like an emptiness, a vacuum, a void. Our teacher calls this the "Big Nothing". It is a very deep state of being which only occurs when we surrender our self-cherishing "I", our identification with our separate self. It is this sense of separation that causes so much suffering and gets in the way on our path homeward. As this begins to dissolve, all the identities that we were attached to can fall away into this vast field of consciousness which is our true nature. This is the true healing, coming home.

Once we are connected to that space, all else begins to fall into place. Jesus asked us to "seek ye first the Kingdom of God... and all else shall be added unto you" (Matthew 6:33). First we must be willing to trust enough to leap into the unknown, out of our normal patterns that keep us (and our voice) bound. We must be willing to leave everything we know behind and to risk the possible chaos that a healing crisis often brings. We must dare to sound bad in the process. This journey, like any other spiritual quest, is about trusting the process – doing our best and leaving the rest. Sound work is like a divine tune up. As we begin to produce these healing frequencies we are lifted into a very fine state of awareness.

According to Weeks, Novalis said "every sickness is a musical problem" (34). We are vibrating light, spirit (energy) that has densified enough to be matter.

When thinking is put aside and we open to what is, we awaken to a whole new way of being. This is a real key: as we get out of our own way we open to a freshness, a wholeness which is here right now awaiting us. God hasn't gone anywhere; it is only we who have gone out to lunch. In the *Marriage of Heaven and Hell*, William Blake speaks of the need to clean the doors of the senses in order to be able to really experience life. In sound work this happens when the brilliances begin to appear and actually cleanse the sense organs, especially the larynx. We come into a new alignment with a cosmic order that creates an inner harmony that will express itself also in our outer lives. When we reactivate our awareness of who we really are, we know ourselves to be in and of God. Jesus said "If therefore thine eye be single, thy whole body shall be full of light" (Matthew 6:22).

Quantum physics research states that our bodies are more than 99% emptiness.[35] That's a lot of spaciousness; certainly more space than matter. We can lean into that and sing from that emptiness, to allow that quality to appear in the sound.

Coming back to these brilliances (singer formants), the first one to appear in the voice is at 3,000 Hz. This is often referred to as the initiation formant. The next two formants (at 5,000 and 8,000 Hz) are stimulated by its energy. On the way to having these appear continuously in the sound, as I have mentioned, there may be a lot of stirring up of old patterns which need to be transformed. These healing frequencies have the capacity to change one's whole structure: the body, breathing, our physical structure right down to the cellular matrix. They literally attune you to the music of the spheres, the cosmic consciousness. The reason they have been called brilliances is because of their similarity to white light (which contains all colours). The voice becomes self organised (which means that there is no application of will from without). The brilliances become the ordering principle, the master of the sound, calling all the other elements of the sound to a higher order.

Brilliances also help connect the left and right hemispheres of the brain – the male and the female aspects – the polarities. This split of polarities into duality can only be healed by returning to the state of oneness. In *The Gospel According to Thomas* (Lambdin), Jesus says:

> *When the inner and the outer, the above and the below, the male and the female become as one single unit... then you enter the kingdom.*

In the *Scientific Healing Affirmations*, Paramahansa Yogananda explains that:

> *Within the gross vibration of flesh is the fine vibration of the cosmic current, the life energy; and permeating both flesh and life energy is the most subtle vibration, that of consciousness.*

* * *

> *The "word" is life energy or cosmic vibrator force. The "mouth of God" is the medulla oblongata in the posterior part of the brain, tapering off into the spinal cord. This, the most vital part of the human body, is the divine entrance ("mouth of God") for the "word" or life energy by which man is sustained.* (13)

Also from the Bible "Man shall not live by bread alone, but by every word that comes from the mouth of God" (Matthew 4:4). The Sufis call this boundless sound *Anahad*. The Hindus have the same word for sound and breath which is *Sura*. They are totally linked. The breath is the life current or *Prana* and the sound is an expression of that. One must be willing to lose her or his identity in order to become a clear channel for the sound. On the path to this high level of sound we open the supersense (which is when all the senses are united and working towards their highest purpose – which is to experience and express the Cosmic Energy).

In conclusion, I would like to share a few quotations in connection to the mysticism of sound from those who are deeply attuned to this state. According to Hafiz, the great Sufi poet from Persia, many say life entered the human body with the help of music, but the truth is that life itself is music. He also says that "It is not known how far is the destination, but this much I know: that music from afar is coming to my ears" (quoted by Khan).[36]

In *The Music of Life* Hazrat Inayat Khan reveals that the "at-one-ment with the Absolute manifests as the music of the spheres" and we experience this in all of life. We are music, music is us (14). These sounds are like a lighthouse guiding us on our way. In *The Sufi Message* he says, "The music of the spheres is the music which is the source of creation" and "it is heard and enjoyed by those who touch the very depth of their own lives".

This is unity consciousness, where there is no longer any doubt of who we are or why we are here. Everything is seen as sacred and interconnected. Sound can be a very powerful tool on the path to this mystical awareness.

The mysticism of sound is about making direct contact with the Infinite through the vehicle of sound; to touch and become aware of that level of being where all is connected. Once we are tuned to the Source we become intuitively self-directed. Our actions are led/guided by our higher self.

Our bodies are nothing but vibrating energy; we are vibrating beings of light. As we allow ourselves to surrender to our highest good and rest in the stillness, we begin to hear these sounds within. Our very body becomes a sacred temple where the sound of the eternal is heard. Extending out from there we begin to hear the voice of the Beloved everywhere: in the cooing of the dove, in the gentle breeze in the treetops, in the roar of the sea. Nowhere is Spirit separate from creation. We then hear/see/feel that presence everywhere. Our life is uplifted to a different level, a higher octave. Our life becomes a song of praise and thanksgiving. Ultimately this is the healing. Once the sense of separation is released we come home to unity consciousness. This is the vision of oneness, the Promised Land, the return to paradise. In understanding the mystical nature of sound we open a powerful doorway to this realisation. Sound then becomes a vehicle first for opening the door to our awareness of the divine and then for expressing our gratitude for our connection to the All. Life becomes a symphony as the cosmic song pours through us; it is all Grace unfolding.

> *Shining, undying,*
> *This glistening Emptiness*
> *Vibrates through all of creation;*
> *It is the shimmering sound of silence.*
> *Trust that. Let it guide you, shine you,*
> *Enlighten you.*

> ~ Shanti

If you can, find time (perhaps linked to your meditative practice) to be with sound just as it is, whether it is inner sound, external sound or your own voice. Resource 9, which contains my notes from a sound work class, may be helpful. Listen without judging, without trying to change anything. Just be with the sounds as vibrations, let them touch you and open you to the vastness of your infinite nature. Allow yourself to sing from that space of emptiness and gratitude. Something magical and yes, even mystical may reveal itself.

CHAPTER SIX: DANCE THROUGH THE DOORWAY – FROM SHANTI WITH LOVE

In dwelling, be close to the land.
In meditation, go deep in the heart…
In action, watch the timing.

~ Lao-Tzu

My spiritual journey has brought me great comfort in life's valleys, transcendent joy at its peaks, and as I wander the slopes and plateaus between in my everyday life, it has brought me much peace and contentment. I want all that for you, for everyone.

I delight in sharing what has inspired me, and this can often be in the

Figure 7. Author with her four children.

form of emails, mainly to my children (Figure 7), other family members and friends, passing on lessons learned or that perfect saying. This chapter is a collection of some of these letters, with a smattering of speaking notes. Now I am offering them to you with love.

Working with Regret

God, grant me the serenity to accept the things I cannot change,
The courage to change the things I can,
And the wisdom to know the difference.

~Reinhold Niebuhr, "Serenity Prayer"[37]

Sent: Monday, January 25, 2010 4:02 PM
Subject: Teachings on regret

These few steps have helped me to work with my own regrets in my life. Perhaps you will also find them useful.

1. First <u>acknowledge</u> and be clear on the situation that you regret. Allow yourself to feel the regret for what you did (or didn't) do.

2. Next, resolve firmly to <u>learn</u> from this and not repeat the same thing again.

3. The next step is to <u>make amends</u> – find a way or ways to atone, to say or write to that person and apologise (or ask for forgiveness) and let them know that you have learned from this incident and are determined to act differently from now on. This step requires you to (when possible) contact the person and say (or write) that you are sorry for any hurt caused by your behaviour. Sometimes it is not appropriate to contact the person (for example someone that we have stolen something from in the distant past). In this case, you can find ways of being generous and kind to others to make up for this unskilful action, being determined not to repeat this kind of action

(whether it is lying, stealing, or hurting another in any way).

Your regret may be about something that you didn't do that you wished you had; here you can find ways of acting thoughtfully and kindly in the present moment and begin now.

If the person is dead or not contactable we can do the same process inside ourselves, as if we were speaking to them. We need to always remember that all things are connected in the great circle of life and what we do now, for anyone, touches the whole biosphere of life.

4. Once we have done what we can to make amends then the next step is very important. Resolve to live in a way that will minimise regrets... Forgive ourselves and others for anything that has happened in the past... Let go... and move on, being the best we can be in the moment and releasing ourselves from our past. The present moment is all we really have and this is where freedom and joy lie.

When Buddha taught the precepts (the mindfulness trainings) he never meant that these things (lying, stealing, using harsh words, taking drugs, having sexual encounters with someone who is with someone else or while we were with someone else) were "wrong" actions, just that they were unskilful because they would usually bring about suffering. He was wise enough to know that when our minds are full of regrets for what we have done, it is very hard to be at peace. Since peace in oneself is the greatest joy, this is what encourages us towards what Buddha calls "right action" or "right speech". But it was always with the awareness that we (like sailors who use the North Star or Southern Cross to guide their boats) use these trainings to set our course right again, doing our best in life but not beating ourselves up when we don't. Funnily enough it is often our suffering that inspires us towards freedom, so-called enlightenment!

The recognition that "suffering is resistance to what is"[38] is a good one. It is very important that when we work with regrets we make efforts to transform that which has caused them, but then forgive ourselves and others so that we can get on with the task of bringing joy into ourselves and the world (rather than continuing to drag around our heavy baggage). Once we see the light and the reason to let go of things, they can fall away easily and we can get on with our lives in a constructive way where we can bring our best to them. Then it is up to us not to go back to behaviours that we know will cause suffering in the long run.

The Dalai Lama says that it is not situations that enslave us; it is our clinging to them.[39] Hence the need to transform and let go.

Buddha says our actions are our "only true belongings" and they have "consequences".[40]

After we have worked with particular regrets (we can take say one a day) and let them go, if a negative state arises in our quiet time (like meditation) we can:

a. Just notice it, say hello to that old friend and let go and move on.

b. If it keeps persisting then we can explore it, be with it, enter into it, look at its layers or just accept it. Deal with it by simply being there for it (for this part of ourselves). If something else needs to be done it will come to us intuitively.

c. If none of this works then do something else – take a walk, a run, a swim, a shower, a cup of tea… change the energy.

Anyway… I hope these are useful for your inner explorations; the work you do on yourself now will free you to live a joyful, meaningful existence that blesses not only you but all of life. We deserve that! In love…

∗   ∗   ∗

Date: Thu, 25 Mar 2010 10:08:10 +1300
Subject: Musings

Hi darlings. I wanted to share with you various thoughts or writings that have inspired me. Last month I sent you a write up I did on working with regrets. I don't know if you found that useful (or even if you read it), but here is another installment.

We can choose to be happier. Here's what's been proven to work:[41]

- appreciation for what others have done for you, especially when shared in a letter;
- counting blessings (once a week, write down at least five things you are thankful for);
- kindness (help others, donate or volunteer);
- positive thinking (for example, envision how you'd like yourself and your life to be, and preferably keep a record);
- listing your strong points and different methods of using them – then giving it a try; and
- meditation.

Studies show that these "positive interventions"/activities work best if you choose those that suit your age and personality, vary them, and strangely, practice each – with the possible exception of meditation – just once a week (for example, five good deeds a week produced more happiness if performed the same day rather than different days). In one study, it helped to begin with writing letters of gratitude, which may inspire one to "pay it forward", but in general, any of these positive activities lead to more and different positive activities. People who put energy into these interventions, and are enthusiastic and expect success will reap the most benefit. And if we let others know their efforts are appreciated, it will increase their well-being too.

The theory is that by taking positive steps to increase our happiness, we will be better prepared to face life's challenges, and may improve our immune systems, careers and relationships.

Here is a summary of Tarchin Hearn's "Recipe for Misery". I find this a good reminder.

1. *Decide you're really dissatisfied with something.*
2. *Focus on it.*
3. *Decide you won't be able to be happy until this changes (or is fixed).* ☹

WAY OUT

1. *Make a decision that you are willing to let go of this.*
2. *Open your eyes; look around. Become aware of what is, in this moment.*
3. *Contemplate the interconnectedness of all of life and appreciate life just as it is, right now.* ☺

I like that, and it works.

As far as I can see, we are here to awaken to the truth of who we are and to live consciously; not to live feeling separate from each other, divided and miserable, but to come to know the interconnectedness of all of life. Nothing is outside of That. Nothing left out. Call it Great Spirit, Life, Love, Source, Emptiness, the Infinite, the All, God, the Whole... it doesn't matter. Names can never describe it; they can only point to it...

Everything exists in That Spaciousness. Everything came from That, lives in That and returns to That. We are never outside of That, it is just veiled from our consciousness because it is obscured by our identification with our body/mind, our things and all that we think of as "ours" or our small separate self. Yet we are that Infinite being appearing as... Everyone and everything is That. We suffer when we think ourselves to be separate from That and from one another. We suffer when we want things to be permanent that are impermanent (like our bodies, our youth, or our loved ones' bodies). We suffer when we resist what is. Because things are always as they are and if we can find a way to flow with them rather than resist them, life transforms. It can become like a prayer.

In *The Power of Now*, Eckhart Tolle suggests living with "joy, ease and lightness" and that this is a choice that we can make every day – to call in these qualities (71). Obviously we need to throw in lots of compassion and understanding for the human condition as well. But have you noticed that we are always happy... when we are not unhappy? Happiness is often kept at bay by clinging to our unhappy stories.

I like that saying that all God ever really wants of you is for you to "be your own unique self".[42] We aren't meant to be carbon copies of anyone else. We each have our gifts and our strengths that we can offer to the world. Rather than compare ourselves with anyone else we can develop the qualities that are ours. Those are our gifts, and they are valuable and worthwhile!

Right now you can, just for a moment, close your eyes, take a few breaths aware of breathing in and aware of breathing out... then put your attention on the space, that vastness that everything is moving in and through. If thoughts are there, let them float through like soft clouds (you can attend to them later). Instead open to the space that is the Source of all that. Give yourself the luxury of stopping even if it is just for two minutes. We can recharge this way... stop, breathe, become aware. Stress and concerns can fall away and joy and lightness can return. Call this mindfulness or call it time out. What is important is to frequently pause and breathe, to just let everything be as it is.

That's all for now... Love you.

* * *

Date: Sun, 18 Nov 2012 09:26:51 +1300
Subject: From Eckhart Tolle

Hi all! A very good writing from Eckhart Tolle, a lot of wisdom in it. Worth sharing and contemplating I reckon, and only a one pager! Love Shanti

THE PAST CANNOT SURVIVE IN YOUR PRESENCE

Whatever you need to know about the unconscious past in you, the challenges of the present will bring it out. If you delve into the past, it will become a bottomless pit: There is always more. You may think that you need more time to understand the past or become free of it, in other words, that the future will eventually free you of the past. This is a delusion. Only the present can free you of the past. More time cannot free you of time.
Access the power of Now...[The Power of Now 90]

You cannot find yourself by going into the past. You find yourself by coming into the present. Past and future are just concepts created by the mind in the present. All you have is right now and each right now is a seed for the next right now. We create our future each moment, as we go. This is a powerful realisation.

Enjoy each Moment

* * *

De-Stressing

Date: Tue, 14 Sep 2010 13:00:54 +1200
Subject: Stress meditation

Hi! Just thought you might like to try this de-stress meditation... very simple.

First just start with a few deep breaths (into the belly), aware of breathing in and aware of breathing out.

Then simply add breathing in..."calm/ease" (same deep breath into the belly), and breathing out "stress" or "all concerns". The inhale can happen naturally followed by a long slow exhale out the mouth with perhaps even a sigh.

Close your eyes and do that for just a few minutes, receiving the calm into your body and letting go on the out breath of all concerns, worries and stress.

Add a wee inner smile if you want your endorphins to kick in and support you as well and that's it!

It works...

* * *

Letting Go /Accepting What Is

Date: Thu, 19 Jul 2012 21:28:58 +1200
Subject: FW: Quote of the Week | Abandon Any Hope of Fruition

Hi,
Just got this quote I thought you might like. It feels very relevant to me.

Lots of love...

> ABANDON ANY HOPE OF FRUITION [43]
> *"Fruition" implies that at some future time you will feel good. One of the most powerful Buddhist teachings is that as long as you are wishing for things to change, they never will. As long as you're wanting yourself to get better, you won't. As long as you are oriented toward the future, you can never just relax into what you already have or already are.*

A mind without conflict is such a great treasure. Peace is truly the greatest joy. A clear conscience and a peaceful heart make it so easy to get to sleep at night.

* * *

Date: Sun, 23 Sep 2012 20:00:04 +1200
Subject: From Lori

Hi... I thought you might enjoy reading this... It was sent by a woman called Lori Deschene who put it together on her 33rd birthday. Quite a lot of wisdom in it...

"33 Things to Accept and Embrace" from tinybuddha.com/blog/.

Among her 33 birthday resolutions, Lori decided to try to accept what is, to let go of her preconceptions about physical attractiveness and the ideal relationship, and to stop striving to be flawless or to please or change others. She wanted to learn to "Accept and Embrace" change and suffering, and to forgive everyone, including herself. Recognise that every life matters and that if we can be grateful for what is, we can free ourselves and others.

Quite a lovely idea, and after reading Lori's list on-line, if you feel inspired, maybe we could each make one of our own?

* * *

Sent: Saturday, 10 August 2013 5:46 PM
Subject: Contemplations

Hi… We are so enjoying our time here in Taizé, singing, walking and time for inner reflection. Today they spoke of how "our faith in God (in the divine) makes us free. It frees us from fear and it frees us for loving service to those who God has entrusted us with". I was just thinking of how our family and friends are "entrusted" to us… And what a privilege it is to be given people to love like that. It brings so much meaning and purpose into our lives as it is a huge job to love really well.

The other contemplation was that "God wants us to be happy" and that "we need not let our worries/concerns and fears suffocate our joy". Such a helpful thing to remember. It was suggested that when we feel worry or anxiety (or whatever) that if we simply note it – "worry" – it can help us see and release this mind pattern and then return to our natural state of joy. In my life I have also made a wee commitment to myself to let go of the "shoulds". Anyway… I just wanted to share that with you as I found it very helpful.

Loving you (PS so glad that you were entrusted to me and I to you…)

Enjoy each Moment.

* * *

Date: Sun, 22 Sep 2013 14:24:29 +1200
Subject: Tidbits of contemplations

Hi there... I am having one of those contemplative moments and I just wanted to share some of it with you as you are all so very dear to my heart.

I will begin with a quote from Eckhart Tolle.

> *When you surrender to what is and so become fully present, the past ceases to have any power... The realm of Being, which had been obscured by the mind, then opens up. Suddenly, a great stillness arises within you, an unfathomable sense of peace. And within that peace, there is great joy. And within that joy, there is love. And at the innermost core, there is the sacred, the immeasurable, That which cannot be named.*

> [*The Power of Now* 229, 224]

This is just so true. I was also thinking about one of the great but simple teachings I received from Swami-Ji in my early twenties that has been a guiding star for me and that was *"Most people believe that if they get what they want they will be happy but I tell you that the truth is that it is the other way around... Just be happy and all the reasons to be happy will start flowing towards you"*.

He gave me so many treasures of wisdom that I took to heart and that have simplified and uplifted my life so much, like the simple one of "Take it as it comes". So much wisdom in that. People worry so much about things that haven't happened yet and so much energy can be lost in the process since "things are as they are".

I would like to encourage you to also let yourself be drawn by the stronger pull of what you really love; you can trust that and be guided by that. Good to also look at where we invest our life energies. It has been said that *the wise person sees all, the light and the shadow, and chooses to affirm the positive*. It is so easy to get caught in the negative, but what does it serve?

When I had lunch at Driving Creek the other day the sign on the wall said "If you want to be happy... be grateful!" That is also so true as being grateful opens the heart and allows us to feel our inner joy where the opposite (complaining about things) actually contracts the petals of the heart and certainly doesn't bring us joy... One last thing I would like to share... My cousins said that my grandparents were always reminding them, which I thought was lovely, "Never give up on people", "Constantly seek for truth" and "Remember that there is nothing constant except change so roll with life". Anyway I hope you enjoy these little tidbits that I offer from my heart to yours; perhaps they may bless you as they have blessed me.

With love and gratitude for your presence in my life.
Shanti

*　*　*

Generosity

Date: Sat, 18 Sep 2010 09:50:53 +1200
Subject: Tithing/ "pay it forward"

Dear ones:
Wanting to share with you today about the joys and benefits of tithing, something the Buddhists call *Dana* which simply means generosity. In all the ancient traditions they have a word for this sense of giving from the heart. Here, the Maori call it *Koha*.

Interestingly, Rainer was reading an article about Bill Gates,[44] who has some amazing amount of money like 50 billion dollars! He has approached all the major billionaires and asked if they would be willing to give half of their wealth to charity. We are talking huge amounts here which would make a big dent in poverty and disease and be such an act of generosity. Well, he has declared that he will give half of all his and Melinda's money and we heard that at least 40 other billionaires have already joined him saying that they will as well. WOW! Isn't that cool! I hope it happens.

As you know, there are so many ways to give of our abundance; yes, money is one of them, but so are time, energy, presence, love, our smile and a kind word. Any "random act of kindness" really.

Tithing traditionally meant giving 10% of what you earn. But really it is just meant to encourage us to know the joy of giving: that when we give, it comes back abundantly in so many different ways (often unexpected). It is said to be the key that opens the door for abundance to flow back towards us.[45]

It has also been said that it is a blessing to receive and even more of a blessing to give.[46]

I don't know if any of you have seen the movie *Pay It Forward*. Really worth seeing. A young boy comes up with a scheme of transforming the world by each person (starting with oneself) doing something big for 3 other people, simply requesting that they "pay it forward" by doing something really nice for 3 other people. So very quickly, this mushrooms: 3 become 9, the 9 become 27, the 27 become 81… etc. Soon the whole planet would be full of people being kind to each other!

As you know, *generosity breeds generosity.*

I know you all have very giving hearts. I am very proud of who you all are and the big hearts that you have. And I also know that we as human beings often hold tight to what we have, rather than opening our hearts and just giving in whatever way we can. So I am just encouraging all of us to consider how we can be even more generous with all the gifts we have. How can we give more back to life? This isn't about depleting ourselves; it's actually about nourishing ourselves through the joy of giving! Let me know what you come up with.

Also… I would recommend seeing that movie; it is quite inspiring to know we have so much transformative power at our fingertips. It starts with us.

What a beautiful planet we have the possibility of creating if that "generous" virus could take hold! And it's contagious!
Lots of love

* * *

Kindness

Date: Sun, 15 May 2011 10:19:55 +1200
Subject: Fw: Tara Dhatu STP. From Prema: A Kind Heart

Dear ZaZa... Did I send this to you? It is so lovely... a good reminder. Thanks for being in my life. Love Shanti

> *A kind heart is the essential cause of happiness. Being kind to others is the nicest thing we can do for ourselves. When we respect others and are considerate of their needs, opinions and wishes, hostility evaporates. It takes two people to fight, and if we refuse to be one of them, there is no quarrel.*
>
> *... A kind heart is the root of harmony and mutual respect. It prevents us from feeling estranged or fearful of others [or] becoming angry, attached, closed-minded, proud or jealous. When opportunities arise to help others we won't lack courage or compassion [If we are wisely cultivating a kind heart].*

--from *Open Heart, Clear Mind* by Thubten Chodron, foreword by His Holiness the Dalai Lama, published by Snow Lion Publications (76).

* * *

Date: Sun, 18 Aug 2014 10:25:10 +1200
Subject: I wish you enough

Dear ones – Here is a beautiful little story Rosie found on Facebook tonight that I want to share with you. It was something overheard at an airport where an old lady was saying goodbye to her daughter. They both just said "I wish you enough" to each other as they parted. Then the old lady turned away and saw this person who was watching them, and told her why they said it, and that it was to always wish each other just enough of the good things in life to sustain them. This was possibly to be their last time together as she was very old and they could not afford to visit each other again.

146

Then she closed her eyes and spoke [the full version of Bob Perks' poem in *I Wish You Enough* that begins]...

> *I wish you enough sun to keep your attitude bright.*
> *I wish you enough rain to appreciate the sun more. ...*

She then began to cry and walked away.[47]

> *They say it takes a minute to find a special person, an hour to appreciate them, a day to love them but then an entire life to forget them.*[48]

* * *

Be a Light Unto Yourself

Date: 18 May 2013
Subject: Be a light unto yourself

Hi all: *This is from a talk I gave on the day of the Last Supper, the Passover feast Jesus shared with his disciples:*

I want to weave into our time together what has been moving me, trusting that this is where we can start today...where we go with it is yet to unfold...

Brother Roger, founder of Taizé, said *"Dare to give your life for others, there you will find meaning for your existence"*.[49] The teachings of Brahma Kumar invite us to come home to the realisation of who we really are. Beyond the egoic consciousness, we are That Light, we are love. Our true nature is joy, stillness, peace. We are reminded by Sister Shalom often, when we meet Wednesdays for our community meditation, that "Our practice here at Dharma Gaia is to be happy". It is a practice that we cultivate by planting seeds of loving kindness and compassion and by letting go of the blockages to that joy.

Many years ago my root teacher said to me, "Your practice, your *sadhana*, is to be ever eternally joyful". For me that also means that all the self-cherishing (or as Tarchin Hearn calls it, the ♫"me, me, me, me"♫) has to be let go. As long as we are full of ourselves there is no room for God or our true Self. In the silence, in the stillness when all else falls away, I am. That presence, that peace is the truth of who I am. Jesus also said, *"Know the truth, and the truth will set you free"* (John 8:32 NIV). That is the real freedom!

If we find that some old story keeps popping up we can use Byron Katie's technique adapted from *Loving What Is* and ask ourselves:[50]

1. *Is it true?*
2. *Can I absolutely know that it is true?*
3. *How do I react when I believe that thought?*
4. *What or who would I be without the thought?*

Or as Adyashanti explains in *Falling into Grace, we suffer because we believe our thoughts,* and thoughts aren't truth, they are just thoughts (5).

> *Change the story and you change perception; change perception and you change the world.*~Jean Houston

Let's look deeply at what wants to be shared today. Who are you...really? What helps create joy, ease and lightness in your life? When we let go of needing things to be a certain way and become empty of all sense of a separate self, then we realise that there is only the One being, appearing as many. Then we can enjoy everyone's uniqueness. When we are no longer concerned with what people think of us, we are getting very close to freedom. Often our idea of freedom has to do with outward appearances, but true freedom is an inside job. The real freedom is not limited by our outward circumstances needing to be a certain way. It just is. I invite you to take a moment to ponder this worthwhile insight.

Let us be aware that this is the evening of the Last Supper. Is there a cross we carry that we may want to lay down, in order to be ready to be a deeper, clearer channel of Spirit? Once we are at peace in ourselves then we can truly be channels (instruments) of peace for others.

What is true freedom to you? How do you live that, share that? Who are you really? Buddha's last words to his disciples as he let go of his body were "Be a light unto yourself". What can support us right now to be that light, that peace? Is there a story we need to let go of, or do we simply need to claim the truth of who we are and be courageous enough to be That, live That?

* * *

(See the questions in Resource 10, and explore some of the topics in the worksheets in Resource 11 (Intentions) and Resource 12 (Explorations).)

The Peace Prayer of St. Francis

Lord make me an instrument of your peace.

Where there is hatred,
Let me sow love;
Where there is injury, pardon;
Where there is error, truth;
Where there is doubt, faith;
Where there is despair, hope;
Where there is darkness, light;
And where there is sadness, Joy.
O Divine Master grant that I may not so much seek to be consoled
As to console;
To be understood, as to understand;
To be loved, as to love.
For it is in giving that we receive,
It is in pardoning that we are pardoned,
And it is in dying that we are born to eternal life.

~ Anon.[51]

CHAPTER SEVEN: COMING HOME (Stories from Life's Learnings)

The struggle ends when gratitude begins.

~Neale Donald Walsch

The Importance of Gratitude

I am so grateful for all the love in my life – so many beautiful beings to love and enjoy. I also feel deeply blessed to have four children, each one so very dear to my heart. You may remember that my spiritual journey began in earnest after I lost my first child to adoption in 1970. I got pregnant at eighteen, the week I left home and the first time I made love. I felt afraid and alone, humbled by the way others saw me. I hid my pregnancy for a long time under baggy sweaters. In those days it was still seen as a disgrace to be an unmarried mother; there was no support emotionally or financially. Then for the last few months my beloved sister welcomed me into her home, as I was afraid to tell my parents. My greatest grief was after I surrendered my child (a heart-wrenching decision that I was persuaded would be best for her) and then tried to get her back and couldn't. I searched desperately for her for years. I even ran a home for young teen mothers called "Threshold" in the early 70's as part of my own healing process and with the intention to support these young women to be able to make a conscious decision, as I felt my own had been unconscious and fear based. Then when I finally found her through an illegal agency, the joy and gratitude that I experienced was indescribable. I was over the moon. My husband will tell you that when I got the phone call in 1991 saying that she had been found, I almost jumped through the roof in rapture. I was higher than a kite for weeks.

It was such a priceless gift to know that she was alive and well, and then later to meet her at a rustic lakeside retreat, to find that her adoptive parents had raised a woman who was as gorgeous inside as out, to get to know her and have her in my life, and to see her with her birth brother and sisters. Of course we have had challenges and issues to deal with and to take care of, but the love is worth it all. Now I have six grandchildren, two of whom are her children. I feel so blessed. The whole family loves her; she will always feel like a bit of a miracle – to have lost her for 21 years and then to find her again. Talk about a heart filled with gratitude.

I have heard that once, long ago, in the time of Lao Tzu, there was an old man who lived alone with his only son at the outskirts of a village. They were very poor but he had a magnificent white horse that was the envy of many. One day the horse disappeared and the whole village gathered saying, "What a misfortune old man, perhaps even a curse, your only possession is gone". The old man simply replied, "Yes, the horse has vanished, this is the fact; everything else is just a judgement. Whether it is good or bad, we don't know. We will see. Meanwhile I give thanks for all my blessings". They thought the old man was a bit crazy. Then, after ten days had passed, the stallion returned with a whole herd of beautiful wild mares. Again the people gathered with their judgements, this time saying what a blessing it was. Again the old man answered in the same way. "Yes, the horse has returned with a whole herd, but please no need to pass judgement, whether this is good or bad is unknown, we will see". The son soon began to tame the wild mares and one day had a bad fall and shattered his leg. The people came, as usual offering their opinions about what a misfortune this was. The old man's answer was always the same, reminding the villagers that this was just a small piece of the whole picture. A month later the country went to war and the military came and enlisted all the young men of the village. Only the old man's son was left. The whole town came, weeping and crying, "You were right old man, this proved to be a blessing, your son may limp but at least you have him with you. Ours are gone perhaps never to return". The old man, with great compassion, simply said, "We will see".

Jane (a dear friend of mine) and I love this small teaching story and often when we find ourselves about to pass judgement about something, we remind each other by saying, "Remember the white horses".

Give thanks for everything. Who can say what is good or bad? We will see.

I have grown to realise that gratitude is a practice that can be cultivated and an attitude that keeps our hearts open and transforms life. It brings so much joy to be in the energy of appreciating: grateful for life, the people we are with and all the richness and learnings that come our way every day.

The North American indigenous people have a practice called "the blessing way". They suggest that this includes *setting a sacred intention for your day, giving thanks and offering at least one life-affirming action daily.* Then your life becomes a blessing way.

We all need to take time to renew, replenish, rejuvenate and come home to ourselves. One of my ways of nourishing myself is singing, especially with our choir, which brings me such joy; there are moments of soaring together where the song sings us. I treasure those moments and am so grateful to have that in my life. People who come to hear us are often transported into that same joy that we are experiencing. That is a wonderful spin-off and blessing.

* * *

I want to share with you my experience of seeing my mother for the last time in her physical body, and how deeply this touched and impacted me, and most of all how much gratitude it filled me with.

At the end of our six days together, when I told my mom that I was leaving in forty minutes, she made some sounds that were so sad I can't even describe them, but they made my heart ache, and then she said "Oh God, no…", in such a similar way to what my Dad uttered as his last words just before he drowned beside me in the ocean. Then she pulled me close to her cheek and kissed me very softly again and again (maybe 25 times). We cried a lot. We both seemed to know that this was our last moment together. We spoke of our love for each other and how we had made every single moment count. Much time had been spent just simply being together, silently looking into each other's eyes, holding hands, doing nothing… We had spoken of many things, mostly of how much we meant to each other and how blessed we were to have each other and to feel so loved.

We never said "see you soon" as I left, just "I love you". When the taxi came and she was wheeled off in her wheelchair to lunch, I felt so much gratitude for the depth we had shared and so much sadness to know her sweet smile and eyes would soon only be a memory.

I am reminded of the line in Kahlil Gibran's writing on love, *"To know the pain of too much tenderness"* (6). Such a gift to feel that much love and that much tenderness with another, especially when it is your (my) mother.

> *Life is so fleeting, so precious,*
> *It is well worth treating everyone*
> *with great kindness and tenderness.*

~Shanti

Mom's Funeral ~April 25th 2005

In honour of Margaret Fisher Fallis (née Ferguson) born March 10th 1920, passed into glory April 21st 2005.

Mom's funeral today. I experienced so many feelings simultaneously. I felt this incredible joy and wanted to shout "You did it Mom!" Joy that she had made the transition surrounded by love and peacefully letting go. Joy that she was free of her worn out old body and ready for new adventures unknown, into the Mystery. Then a huge flood of sadness would come, knowing that I wouldn't see, hear or touch her again in this realm. Then gratitude for all she had given me. The moment when she actually passed, Rainer and I were on a boat in Tahiti with all our family, and we were holding hands, doing a *Powa* practice[52] (seeing her dissolving in the light), when Rainer had a very powerful vision of the light embracing her. Then the phone went off in his pocket and it was my siblings to say that she had just passed. Peacefully she had surrendered, no resistance, just the breath slowly stopping. My sister Penny and brother Dave were each holding one of her hands, holding her in love while she made this great transition to the other side.

From my heart I thank you mom…you will always be with me.

* * *

I'd like this Rumi poem, translated by Coleman Barks, to be true for me on my deathbed.

> *At the end of my life,*
> *with just one breath left,*
> *if you come then, I'll sit up and sing.* (95)

Forest Walk ~ May 2005
(Written just after my mother died)

Walking in the forest today, marveling at the beauty and abundance of mushrooms popping up everywhere. In the 22 years that I have lived and walked on this land I have never seen so many – so colourful, fragile and impermanent. What a miracle this life is. I walk on contemplating the recent passing of my mother and finding a new level of "being" with her; recognising that every cell of my body contains her DNA, she truly lives on in me. My eyes open wider, my senses expand as I realise that as I enjoy this wonderful moment of beauty and joy, she continues to enjoy through me. What a wonder, this interbeing. Nothing ever dies, it just transforms. Soon I will sprinkle some of her ashes around the Sanctuary here on the land and her earthly body will become part of the plants and trees and even these mushrooms. I look at the mushrooms and smile. Hi Mom! You're everywhere now!

At the Cottage to Sprinkle our Mother's Ashes ~ May 1st 2006

(In 1919, a memorial to Walt Whitman was carved into the face of Bon Echo Rock at Mazinaw Lake, where my father built our cottage when I was two. As an Air Force family ever on the move, this cottage in the Canadian wilderness was our true home. Accessible only by boat, I found such peace and solace there. We had no electricity; I had a wind-up record player, and certainly no television or any of the devices that fill our world now. Chipmunks and a skunk were my pets and I swung in the treetops with my adventurous brothers and shared secrets with my beloved sister. I remember lying in my cozy bed listening to the inner hum and the lap of the waves. This was my sacred ground as a child, a place where my soul felt so at home, so nourished.)

My foothold is tenon'd and mortised in granite.
I laugh at what you call dissolution.
And I know the amplitude of time. (36)

~Walt Whitman

We walked out to McDowell Lake (Dave, Penny, Rainer and I), a beautiful, silent and secluded spot about 6 km from Mazinaw where the ashes of both my brother Bob and father Keith had been laid to rest many years ago.

After some prayers and a reading we sprinkled my mother's ashes in the lake and around the place we had hiked to so often as children, throwing them to the wind, water and earth with great thanks and love. Suddenly we realised that brother Dave was in so much pain with his leg that he could hardly walk, dragging his right foot. We all helped to carry him out the long distance back to where the car was and rushed straight to the hospital. It turned out that he had an infection that had spread into the bone and was beginning to poison his body. He ended up in Kingston Hospital (for 10 weeks!). They said that if he had been even a day later he would have lost his leg. A week later and he would have lost his life.

Meanwhile Penny had a painful ulcer in her left eye and couldn't see with that eye. It was a very very intense time. Even Uncle Don, whose cottage we were staying at, was in the hospital.

The cottage was beautiful and the bay empty as it was when we were young. The night before we had all walked together around the still bay. The sky was radiant blue and the loons must have just returned; their mournful cries echoed back and forth across the lake like we had never heard before. A wonderful salute to our amazing mom.

Dance through the Doorway
Empty handed,
Open hearted,
Radiant and Free.

~Shanti

Let Us Dance and Sing with Joy

A poem I wrote for Rainer after a *Vipassana* course in August 1984:

I came from the forest;
The mist surrounded me,
Quietly enfolding me like your Love.
Suddenly you were there
Softly, floating like a vision, a dream;
And then you vanished
As I know you will, one day
When the sweet wings of death embrace you.
But while the sun of life is shining
Let us dance and sing with joy;
Then when the mists of death do enfold us
We can lie down and go in peace.

After that retreat and 10 days of silence, during which Rainer and I had been sleeping in separate rooms, we met outside the gate and Rainer brought me a deep red rose. His first words in 10 days were "Will you marry me?" We were already married and pregnant but I felt so much love (from him, for him and a huge well-spring in my own heart). May the boundaries of our love never be found.

Shining Star

I composed this poem for my youngest daughter Tanya's 19th birthday, in December 2003.

Our prayers were answered:
She came to us in the early spring, when all around new life
did sing.
Her angel appeared at 4 and taught her to love...even

more.
When she was 6 she found her lost sister, from wishing on
stars, she knew she had missed her.
At 11, she lost her brother (just for a day), that was when
love taught her to really pray.
She loved to speak German with her dad, and for that he
was very, very glad.
When she was 16 she wanted to try her wings and before
we knew it she was off to Kings.
That was the year Sam came into her life and perhaps, who
knows, one day she may be his wife.
She's beautiful and bright, filling our lives with her
precious light.

Gleaming Waters

Rainer is an obstetrician, and I had always dreamed of being a midwife. In the 1980's, he and I were blessed to work together as a team offering home births for friends, neighbours and of course, ourselves. Each experience of birthing was intense, often verging on the sublime at that moment when infinity opens wide and enters this world of matter, filling us with reverence and awe. Birthing is certainly not without its challenges and sometimes very fraught moments, but we felt so privileged to be ushered into these deeply intimate experiences.

My own births were huge milestones in my life. I will just share a wee snippet of my fourth and final birthing experience. We were walking in the forest when my contractions started. The full moon was just beginning to rise over the mountain. I came inside dancing, singing, feeling the primordial power of the universe instinctively surging through me. Later I held onto my husband's strong shoulders and just let the gravitational pull move through me. I felt open, raw, wild, alive and empowered! As my son Sasha burst into the world, it was dark, magical, and his eyes shone of the other world. I fell into them, loving him, knowing him. The stillness of the night wrapped us up in wonder; I felt so content, so ecstatic, so filled with love. My mother cut the cord, then my beautiful daughter Kyla helped to gently bathe him. My rapturous exhaustion was beginning to overwhelm me, but I felt I had touched the absolute glory of womanhood. This peak experience had rewired my internal understanding and appreciation of being woman. I was filled with gratitude as I curled around his tiny body and surrendered to sleep.

New Moon ~ March 2006

As a woman, you are said to be a crone after thirteen moons have passed since your last bleed. This is a poem I wrote then.

I stand to be croned.

Today the new moon and a total solar eclipse support Rosie and I as we claim our wise woman within. 13 Moons have passed since my last bleed.
Many years ago my spiritual teacher said "Shanti your practice (your sadhana) is to be ever eternally joyful". I now breathe into that and fully claim it as true.
No more children's schedules to keep, no more mountains of wash, even the rhythm of my cycle is gone. My emotional body free of the hormonal storms. There is freedom to find and follow my spacious inner flow and I intend to.
I stand to be croned.

Now a woman who holds her blood, her energy, her power within. Ready to embark willingly on the next phase of this journey.
This is the autumn of my life. How beautiful this moment, this chapter of this life.
Exactly 13 moons ago on the new moon in March 2005, I bled for the last time (unknowingly). It was my mother's

85th birthday. The next month she passed over and my bleeding never returned. Now I am a grandmother. It is time.
I stand to be croned.

My life is my joy: my song, my dance, my offering into each moment all the love that I can, from my heart. To breathe and to smile. To remember my interconnectedness with all of life. This is a time of letting go, of dissolving.
My reproductive years ~ gone.
My youth ~ gone.
My wisdom ~ right here!
I stand to be croned.

* * *

When we know who we are, we can be the Infinite and still be fully embodied and engaged with life. Like a tuning fork, the resonance that we carry affects everyone around us. The invitation is to keep attuning to grace and opening into the unknown, the mystery. As we let go of our need to know, we are guided. Being love, we attract love. With this awareness, we don't get lost in the layers of old traumas; we learn to navigate so that if these layers arrive in our field we can be with them without needing to identify with them. Then instead of seeing the world through our stories we can just keep opening, expanding and being the embodiment of love.

Guided by the shining presence within
I open my arms to Life.
May my heart be vast enough to hold the world
With tenderness and compassion
For this human condition.
Anchored in Love
I bow down to kiss the ground.

~ Shanti

Johannesburg ~ 2007
(Singing with the black Africans in South Africa)

Shining eyes,
Bright white toothed smiles,
Big hearts, small shacks;
Humbling.
Singing, gratitude.
Mama Flow dancing.
Making us a delicious meal
In her tiny home.
Toilets outside, BYO toilet paper.
Jo's tears in the church;
A melting heart
To hold the world.

* * *

Angeles Arrien claims that we are all members of the "scar clan" (78). No one is immune to the wounds of living here in a body on planet Earth. As we call the disowned parts of ourselves home we become whole. When we attend to even one wound we attend to all. There have often been many traumas in our lives which can feel never-ending if we are attempting to heal each one separately. However, if we expand our consciousness, it is possible to hold them all in our hearts and not be dragged down by our past hurts. Then we can begin to abide in love, in the soul, where there are no borders and no boundaries. This is the place of true healing. Staying anchored in the heart we can sense our truest self. We can then keep coming home to that state of grace where there is nothing to do or fix, nowhere to go. All parts of our human condition are welcome here.

* * *

Many indigenous cultures have recommended ways to help us reconnect with our joy and our inner aliveness by asking ourselves:

- When did we stop singing (for singing is a swift access to joy)? What would help us to find our voice again?
- When did we stop dancing (being really embodied)? What would support us now to be fully alive?
- When did we stop being enchanted by life (filled with wonder and awe)? Can we find our way back to that magical child inside?
- When did we lose our connection to silence, to nature? How can we create space in our lives to be nourished by this soul food?

* * *

Today I needed to feel my body alive,
I needed movement, joy and song
To cleanse me...to refresh me.
You came to me and danced me whole;
You sung through me.
My eyes were filled with the shimmering
moon,
My ears knew nothing but the inner
cicada sounds.
Nothing else...it's as simple as that.

~Shanti

* * *

Letter to Myself
(for a workshop in 2006)

Dear Shanti;

Your spiritual teacher told you many years ago to be "ever eternally joyful", that that was your practice, your *sadhana*. So, dear one, don't be shy; sing, dance, delight in life and don't hold back. I mean really sing, really dance and bring blessings to others by being your own unique self so that they too may be encouraged to be their own authentic selves.

Give yourself the silence and inner time that you love, balancing that with connecting with your loved ones, family and friends. I know you have found that there is such freedom when you can attempt to accept everyone and everything just as they are.

When you walk, you know how it feels to walk steps of peace, moving mindfully and easily like the breeze. Then everything feels spacious and interconnected. Let nature nourish you.

Allow your children to walk their own path. Offer them love and encouragement but don't lead or push.

Trust your life. Go with the flow! Don't plan too much, leave space for the unexpected (the magical), and above all enjoy yourself and you will then naturally be an inspiration for joy in others' lives.

Your seeking days are over; be a finder. Just be here, present to what is. Trust your inner knowing and let it guide you and encourage others to trust theirs. Don't give too much notice to the monkey mind; it is just doing its thing. Instead put your attention on the Space, the expansive Love that is your essential self. Feed that, nourish that and all will be well.

PS. You are doing great and I love you dearly. xx Shanti

PPS. Let your light shine ~

The Buddha has indicated that if *you travelled the world over you would not find anyone more worthy of your love than yourself.*

* * *

Clouds dancing
through an empty sky,
and here am I,
Eternity dancing
through time.

~Shanti~

RESOURCE 1: MY OWN PERSONAL KEYS TO WELL-BEING

I am often asked how I stay so healthy and fit, so I thought I would include some wellness tips that work for me. I try to listen to my body, to sleep when I am tired, and eat when I am hungry, to give the body some movement and exercise every day, and to follow my joy.

- I am usually in bed before 10 pm and get a good 8 hours of sleep.[53] (If you have trouble getting enough sleep, some tips in *Catch the Tide* might help.[54]) I have to add that I am so blessed that my partner gives me a back massage every night as I snuggle into bed. ☺
- Giving and receiving regular massages is such a blessing; to watch and to feel loved ones relaxing under your touch is a joy. All my grandchildren love to sit on my lap and wait for Grammy to get the message.
- I rise early, and do a 45-second dry skin brush[55] to stimulate circulation and eliminate toxins.
- I drink a litre of lemon water before breakfast, a wellness tip I adopted from Cameron Diaz. If there are no lemons on my tree then I use organic cider vinegar. This flushes the system and helps to keep my acid/alkaline balance at a neutral pH of 7, which is where the body likes it. This balance supports the immune system to keep disease at bay. You can read more about this important balance.[56] Under-the-tongue strips to test your own pH balance are available from most health stores.
- Meanwhile every morning before breakfast I do an hour of meditation and yoga/*pranayama* (see the sample meditation instructions in Resource 2 and the breathing exercises in Resource 3 if you are interested). I love the aliveness and the calm this brings to my whole being. As I age I just feel more and more flexible and really enjoy having these practices which

165

support inner and outer well-being. If you can't spare an hour, even 10 minutes a day can make a difference.

- Since our children left home, my partner and I enjoy staying in silence until breakfast – we usually sing some Taizé chants to complete our meditation time just before breakfast. Doing what you love so enhances well-being, and I love to sing.

- We eat mainly whole and organic food, much of which comes from our gardens and fruit trees.[57] This serves to keep us radiant with health. Since I am a vegetarian I do take a B vitamin daily and make sure to get plenty of Omega 3.

- For cold and flu prevention, if someone around me has a bug I will take an extra dosage of Vitamin C and a shot of Echinacea with Goldenseal as preventative medicine. I use natural medicines wherever possible for myself and my family.

- Being aware of what I "consume" (read, watch or listen to) helps keep my energy vibrant. It is important to take responsibility for this as it is a proven fact that what we take in through all of our senses has a big effect on well-being and attitude.[58]

- A real key to wellness is to move these bodies of ours. Most days I walk in nature and roll up the rug and dance Ceroc or Rock & Roll with my partner, or spend time in my garden. I also have a stationary bike which is great for stormy days. Check out the movie *Alive Inside*[59] to see how much impact movement can have also on the elderly. I love to move, but if you aren't so keen or just need more motivation, then you could get yourself an activity tracker,[60] a fun and stimulating way to inspire you to move. Two of my daughters have Fitbits®[61] and really enjoy them.

- I love to sing and am part of a choir that has been singing together regularly for 24 years (since 1992). This brings me (all of us) immense joy, keeps me feeling very alive, and inspires me to sing every single day.

- Most days I make a smoothie with kale from the garden, chia seeds, goji berries, flax, pumpkin seeds, fresh fruit, etc. This always gives me a burst of energy which often I need around 11 in the morning or in the late afternoon. There are many excellent juicers and blenders on the market. I have a NutriBlaster^{TM} [62] which retains all the goodness of the pulp, is easy to clean and use, and grinds up even the smallest seeds in no time.

- I frequently pause during the day to empty out, to mindfully breathe, and to appreciate the beauty and people around me. The simple practice of mindfulness in everyday activities such as brushing your teeth or eating a meal, and just being fully present to what you are doing in the moment, brings a calm sense of serenity into one's day.

- I grew up with the saying that laughter is the best medicine. I am uplifted with being in the company of good friends where laughter is always nearby. Never get so busy that you don't have enough time to be with those you love. Nothing is worth that loss.

- Make sure to ask for forgiveness where needed, and do not leave unfinished business that can keep you from sleeping well at night. Being in right relationship to the people in our lives contributes hugely to our joy and well-being.

- Focusing on what is working in our life, rather than what is not working, keeps us positive and glowing.

- We like to end our days with some stretches on the floor: a group of exercises called Somatics[63] that helped save my husband from needing to get his spine operated on.

- Our stretches are followed by a meditation together (to get started you can use a really great app called Headspace[64]), or we might just sit breathing, enjoying the twilight as it creeps in around us and then soak in a hot tub under the stars. Often, immersed in the warmth and surrounded by the night's beauty, we take the opportunity to share what we are grateful for... a lovely end to the day. If sleep eludes me, I find this simple practice has me "sawing logs" in no time: breathing in deeply four counts, holding for seven and then out through the mouth for eight (5 times) followed by just saying thank you…thank you…thank you.

I know that being in a loving relationship with my partner is incredibly supportive to well-being, as are my relationships with the rest of my family and friends and my beautiful grand-children. Gratitude[65] and contentment all serve to keep the energy alive and fresh. I find giving thanks throughout my day, as well as just before I rise and just before I sleep, brings me much peace. I feel so blessed.

Above all, trust life and follow your bliss. Know what brings you joy and make sure to weave a good amount of that into your day.

There may even be one of these practices that inspires you, that you might want to try to incorporate into your day. Having fun, following your joy and creating wellness are also contagious! May you be well… May you be happy…

RESOURCE 2: MEDITATION INSTRUCTIONS
(Examples)

Let's take a moment to make sure the body is comfortable. Whether you choose to sit on a chair or cross legged on the floor, make sure that the spine is straight but not rigid, hands relaxed and a wee inward smile on the lips.

- Meditation is simply coming home, resting and just being.

- In the stillness of meditation we can get a glimpse, a taste of the vast luminous being that is our true nature and a sense of interconnectedness (interbeing) with all of life.

- Close the eyes. Sit bright, awake and effortlessly. Let us begin by becoming aware of breathing. Aware of breathing in and aware of breathing out. "Breathing in I calm my body…breathing out I smile" [66] to life. Consciously relax down through the body (face, jaw etc.). Letting go… this is really all you need. Enjoy.

* * *

You may want to explore other possibilities.

- You can put your attention on the point between the brows, often called the seat of the soul, awakening the inner seeing, effortlessly resting in that stillness…

- In the same way we can attune to the inner hearing by listening to what is often called "the audible sound current".[67] It is always there. You might hear it like inner cicadas or a conch shell, or tinkling bells. Rest in That… Allow it to nourish and carry you…

- You can also become aware of your inner body…sensing inner aliveness. Perhaps in your palms… We are vibrating beings of light.

Rest in that light, that spaciousness. The ancient *Vedas* say "Thou art That". Let thoughts come and go like clouds in a big empty sky. No need to focus on them. Instead put your attention on the Space/the spaciousness. Relax into that effortlessly. Nothing to do, nowhere to go, nothing to be... Simply a vast field of awareness... Relax into that unified luminous field that is the underlying reality of the whole universe.

- If the mind is busy with thoughts or if emotions arise, welcome it all and return to being aware of breathing in and breathing out... Let that be an anchor, a touchstone. You can consciously breathe out whatever is not serving you. Let the in-breath happen naturally, whereas the out-breath can be long and slow through the mouth, possibly accompanied by a sigh.

A poem by Lao-Tzu advises, "Empty yourself of everything...." Just be with that stillness, your Source/essence... let go into That. That Presence. As Eckhart Tolle says in *The Power of Now*, "To know yourself as the being underneath the thinker, the stillness underneath the mental noise, the love and joy underneath the pain, is freedom, salvation, enlightenment" (154).

Then as we come to the last few minutes of our sit, let us consciously dedicate/offer whatever peace and inner well-being that we have generated through our practice today. In gratitude we offer it out as a blessing in all directions to our family, our friends, and our world.

We can continue to tune into that spaciousness that we are (perhaps sensing the inner sound or inner aliveness). *If we want, we can take that sense of stillness, of being in the centre of radiant consciousness, into the rest of our day, frequently pausing and mindfully breathing.

May all beings be well. May they be happy. May they know peace.

RESOURCE 3: SOME BEGINNER'S *PRANAYAMAS*

Deep breathing techniques can have major health benefits and also bring about deep relaxation and even altered states of consciousness. They are designed to maximise the flow of *prana* (vital force) in the body. Make sure to sit with your spine erect. These exercises are best done on an empty stomach.

Here are a few good ones to get started with:

1.   *Nadi Sodan* (alternate nostril breathing)

Begin by closing your right nostril with the thumb of your right hand and slowly exhale through your left nostril. Then slowly inhale through the same nostril. Hold your breath for 2 seconds. Next close your left nostril with the ring finger of the same (right) hand and exhale through the right nostril. Now, inhale again through that same nostril and hold for two seconds, then exhale through the left one, closing your right nostril again with the right thumb. Begin with an equal inhale/exhale ratio. Repeat the process for 2 to 5 minutes.

This first exercise is very relaxing and balancing for the whole system and is said to improve your eyesight and memory, and to normalise blood pressure as well as aid blood purification.

2.   *Bhastrika Pranayama* (bellows breath)

In this exercise, you're breathing through the nose, but the breath is loud like a burning furnace of fire. It makes a throaty sound.

Start with a deep breath in, where you expand your stomach. Then force the breath out completely by a quick sucking of your tummy towards the spine. Then as you naturally inhale again your belly should expand to the maximum. When ready, increase the speed. Do this for 1-2 minutes and then sit quietly for a while.

Exercise two is said to strengthen the lungs, help with asthma by clearing your windpipe, burn excess fat and strengthen the belly, while improving your mental capacities and even relieving migraines.

3.   *Kapalabhathi Pranayama* (breath of fire)

Breathe in normally and fully and then actively exhale, strongly. During the exhalation the stomach muscles are pulled in as close to the spine as you can get, then let the inhale happen naturally. The belly will be pumping continuously.

This third exercise is said to release toxins as well as reduce belly fat and make it easier to lose weight. It may also improve circulation and the functioning of the inner organs, as well as balancing the blood sugar levels.

That is probably plenty to start with. Take it easy at first and build up your time spent on each exercise as it feels right. You can just start with one of the exercises. These are powerful tools so no need to force anything. If you can, it is always useful to end with a few moments of quiet to feel the body alive. Enjoy.

I would love to hear how you go with this or any of the other Resources.

RESOURCE 4: PERSONAL RETREATS

A retreat can be as simple as time away at your cottage/bach or spending a weekend camping in the forest, or a more structured time spent nourishing your well-being or looking deeply at your life. It is always a gift to yourself. If it is useful for you, here are a few suggestions and guidelines for beginning one of those more structured personal retreats.

It is always beneficial to clarify your motivation. Are you doing this retreat to just relax and rejuvenate? Or do you want to deepen your spiritual practice, receive insight into a certain area of your life, or simply to give yourself some deep inner nourishment? Or it may be all of the above. Good to be clear.

If possible take a day to unwind and settle in, gather some resources and prepare yourself for your inward journey.

There are a few books I could recommend as companions such as Eckhart Tolle's *Practicing the Power of Now,* Thomas Moore's *Care of the Soul,* or Pema Chodron's *Start Where You Are.* Some teaching CDs can also be useful to listen to during your retreat: Eckhart Tolle's *Living the Liberated Life* or his *Realisation of Being;* or Stephanie Dowrick's *Guided Meditations* and many others.

I recommend spending long periods of your day in silence and contemplation. Eating in silence can also be a special delight, as you find that you can really taste every bite. On traditional retreats one often alternates sitting and mindful walking throughout the day. You may want to wander in the bush, or find a hammock or a tree to sit under. Perhaps you might even find going to the top of a mountain inspires you to take a broader view on your life, or to see things from a new perspective.

- You can explore walking silently in nature or doing a yoga session or meditation, as this can support your process immensely.

- You might want to create a ritual for yourself that acknowledges this as a transformational time and find a meaningful way to express that.
- Consider a journal to draw or write insights in.
- Booking in for a massage can aid the body/mind to unwind and let go, particularly at the beginning of, or just before, your retreat.
- Use whatever supports you to deepen into yourself.

Some contemplations to possibly explore, either on your own or with a kindred spirit:

- What is my heart's desire?
- What gives my life meaning?
- How could I cultivate more gratitude in my life and express it more?
- How can I express my gratitude daily?
- What have I learned of truth and how truthfully have I learned to live?
- What have I learned of love and how well have I learned to love?
- How can I be more generous with my time, energy, resources and love?
- What have I learned about tenderness, vulnerability, intimacy and communion?
- What have I learned about courage, strength, power and faith?
- What have I learned of the human condition, and how deep is my compassion?
- How am I handling suffering?
- What helps me to open my heart, empty my mind and experience the presence of Spirit?

- What will give me strength and peace as I die?
- If I remembered my breaths were numbered, how would I relate to breathing right now?
- How can I best share what I have learned? How can I best be of service?

More contemplations if you wish to continue to explore:

- What makes me feel alive? What is really important to me?
- Joseph Campbell recommends following our bliss (xxiv). Am I following mine?
- What are my real gifts? How do I express and share these gifts?
- How do I nurture myself and others?
- How am I enriched by friendship?
- Do I live from a place of gratitude and appreciation or do I get caught in wanting things to be different?
- What does it mean to live wholeheartedly? Am I experiencing this quality in the way I live?
- What is my biggest challenge and how am I working with this at the moment?

At the end of the day as you look back and review, you can inquire:

- What am I grateful for today?
- Where did I offer kindness and support?
- What was life-enhancing?
- Did I love fully and wholeheartedly?
- Where did I hold back?
- What was great about my day? What was challenging?

RESOURCE 5: MANA'S MISSION, VISION AND GUIDING PRINCIPLES

MANA MISSION STATEMENT

Mana is a sanctuary nestled in the bush-covered hills of the Coromandel Ranges. It is a registered charitable trust (1988), established for the exploration and awakening of consciousness, the unfolding of our creative and healing potential and the realisation of our essential unity.

MANA'S VISION

Though rich in spirituality, Mana is not aligned with any one particular religion or spiritual teaching but seeks to embrace and honour all. Mana's vision is to bring together diverse traditions and teachings in healing, spirituality, lifestyle, healthy cuisine etc., celebrating diversity to inspire and nurture peoples' own philosophy.

Mana honours its interbeing with the natural world and views health as the harmonious interaction between a person's physical, emotional and spiritual dimensions.

Mana seeks to educate and support people in their quest for greater health, vitality and the dynamic integration of body, mind and spirit. Mana's spirit of the land and the synergy of its holistic therapies and practices can activate the inner healing power, or life force, within each person and restore a sense of interconnectedness with all of life. This is the ultimate source of all true healing.

GUIDING PRINCIPLES

At Mana we find it inspiring to have some guiding principles which are loving kindness, transformation, generosity, interconnectedness, courage, service, compassion, trust, respect, caring for the environment, dependability, direct communication, integrity, commitment, perseverance, enthusiasm and mindfulness. Staying aware of these principles by revisiting them regularly helps to keep us on track.

When you do things from your soul, you feel a river moving in you, a joy!

~ Rumi[68]

RESOURCE 6: FINDING THE STILL POINT

Questions to consider on the journey to the still point:

1. What do you need to "clear up" in order to be more peaceful?
2. What is needed to experience true peace? What practices would support that?
3. Do you have a designated space in your home for meditation and inner reflection?
4. Are you able to be in the moment, to let things go and just be with what is?
5. What helps you to slow down and be present?
6. Can you pause throughout your day and connect with your breath?
7. How do you re-centre yourself?
8. What holds you back? What might you need to let go of?
9. Why are you here? What have you come to offer, to share?
10. Where is silence/stillness? How do you access it?
11. What transformation is possible for you right now?

If something is knocking you off your centre and you have lost the awareness of that still point within, here is a simple way to return.

    A. Awareness: just become aware of the feeling (i.e. frustration).

    B. Breathe: take a few conscious breaths.

    C. Choice: remember, you always have a choice how to respond.

Let this simple "ABC" practice be a reminder and a tool for finding the still point.

RESOURCE 7: "BEGINNING ANEW"

The following is the lovely practice entitled "Beginning Anew" which inspired "Four Steps to Reconnect" in the chapter on "The Dance of Relationships". "Beginning Anew" is reproduced by the kind permission of Thich Nhat Hanh and Unified Buddhist Church Publishing. Read more about when and how this practice is used at Plum Village, France at pvfhk.org/index.php/en/studies-practices/29-transcripts/dt- (Appendix 7). If you are fortunate enough to attend a retreat at this fourfold *sangha*, as we were, you may find "Beginning Anew" in your orientation booklet.

1) Flower watering - This is a chance to share our appreciation for the other person. We may mention specific instances when the other person said or did something that we had admired. This is an opportunity to shine light on the other's strengths and contributions to the sangha and to encourage the growth of his or her positive qualities.

2) Sharing regrets - We may mention any unskillfulness in our actions, speech or thoughts that we have not yet had an opportunity to apologize for.

3) Expressing a hurt - We may share how we felt hurt by an interaction with another practitioner, due to his or her actions, speech or thoughts. (To express a hurt we should first water the other person's flower by sharing two positive qualities that we have [truly] observed in him or her. Expressing a hurt is often performed one on one with another practitioner rather than in the group setting. You may ask for a third party that you both trust and respect to be present, if desired.)

4) Sharing a long-term difficulty & asking for support- At times we each have difficulties and pain arises from our past that surface in the present. When we share an issue that we are dealing with we can let the people around us understand us better and offer us the support that we really need.

Excerpt from Thich Nhat Hanh's orientation booklet "How to Enjoy Your Stay in Plum Village".

Freedom is not given to us by anyone;
We have to cultivate it ourselves,
It is a daily practice.

~ Thich Nhat Hahn

Southern Hemisphere Medicine Wheel

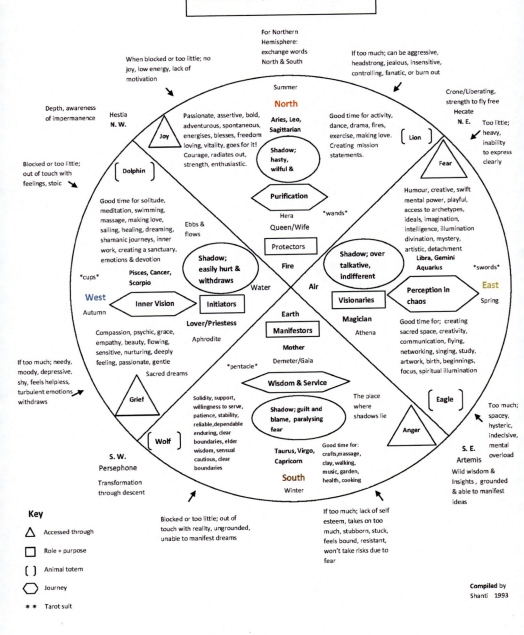

When blocked or too little; no joy, low energy, lack of motivation

For Northern Hemisphere: exchange words North & South

If too much; can be aggressive, headstrong, jealous, insensitive, controlling, fanatic, or burn out

Depth, awareness of impermanence

Hestia N. W.

Joy

Summer

North

Passionate, assertive, bold, adventurous, spontaneous, energises, blesses, freedom loving, vitality, goes for it! Courage, radiates out, strength, enthusiastic.

Aries, Leo, Sagittarian

Shadow; hasty, wilful &

Good time for activity, dance, drama, fires, exercise, making love. Creating mission statements.

Crone/Liberating, strength to fly free

Hecate N. E.

Lion

Too little; heavy, inability to express clearly

Fear

Blocked or too little; out of touch with feelings, stoic

Dolphin

Good time for solitude, meditation, swimming, massage, making love, sailing, healing, dreaming, shamanic journeys, inner work, creating a sanctuary, emotions & devotion

Ebbs & flows

Hera Queen/Wife

Purification

wands

Humour, creative, swift mental power, playful, access to archetypes, ideals, imagination, intelligence, illumination divination, mystery, artistic, detachment

Protectors

cups

Pisces, Cancer, Scorpio

Shadow; easily hurt & withdraws

Fire

Water

Air

Shadow; over talkative, indifferent

Libra, Gemini Aquarius

swords

West

Inner Vision

Initiators

Earth

Visionaries

Perception in chaos

East

Autumn

Lover/Priestess

Spring

Compassion, psychic, grace, empathy, beauty, flowing, sensitive, nurturing, deeply feeling, passionate, gentle

Aphrodite

Manifestors

Mother

Demeter/Gaia

Magician

Athena

Good time for; creating sacred space, creativity, communication, flying, networking, singing, study, artwork, birth, beginnings, focus, spiritual illumination

If too much; needy, moody, depressive, shy, feels helpless, turbulent emotions withdraws

Sacred dreams

Grief

pentacle

Wisdom & Service

Shadow; guilt and blame, paralysing fear

The place where shadows lie

Eagle

Too much; spacey, hysteric, indecisive, mental overload

Anger

Wolf

Solidity, support, willingness to serve, patience, stability, reliable, dependable enduring, clear boundaries, elder wisdom, sensual cautious, clear boundaries

Taurus, Virgo, Capricorn

South

Winter

Good time for: crafts, massage, clay, walking, music, garden, health, cooking

S. E. Artemis

Wild wisdom & Insights , grounded & able to manifest ideas

S. W. Persephone

Transformation through descent

Blocked or too little; out of touch with reality, ungrounded, unable to manifest dreams

If too much; lack of self esteem, takes on too much, stubborn, stuck, feels bound, resistant, won't take risks due to fear

Key

△ Accessed through

▢ Role + purpose

[ ] Animal totem

⬡ Journey

* * Tarot suit

Compiled by Shanti 1993

RESOURCE 9: SOUND WORK CLASS NOTES

Certain sounds create a sense of connectedness, ease, joy and spaciousness when we hear them. Among these sounds are the singer formants or brilliances, specific high frequency sounds that can appear in our voice through the kinds of practices taught at Lichtenberg. Part of their magic is that the relationships between these brilliances (at frequencies of 3,000, 5,000, 8,000 and 13,000 Hz) are in sacred proportions – approximately a golden ratio of 1:1.618.

These sacred proportions and even these specific frequencies are all around us in nature. The sounds emitted by bees, cicadas, and sometimes dolphins, for example, vibrate at 3,000, 5,000 and 8,000 Hz respectively. And the resonant properties of the human ear peak at about 3,000 Hz in our outer ear, 5,000 in our inner ear and 8,000 in the brain stem. These frequencies are healing, and the reason is thought to be because they are in harmony with sacred geometry. For reference, the normal singer's voice has as its highest fundamental sound about 1,500 Hz.

The brilliances / high frequencies are not to be confused with overtones, which use pressure and are split off from the fundamental pitch. The brilliance is part of the sound and in fact can begin to master the sound.

Singing with this awareness needs to be without control or pressure. It can only be allowed – by exploring and becoming aware of these frequencies. To do this we need to become present and available, to begin to sense a spaciousness, an emptiness, what our teacher calls "the Big Nothing". As we open all our senses to this sensory singing we become aware of this luminous field of sound and light. We are all just vibrating beings, so to attune our energy bodies to these divine proportions is to realise our connection with everything.

Can we begin to listen in a new way? Without labels or judgements, just listen to the sound as it is, as vibration, nothing else.

When we sing together as a choir we always begin by creating the awareness of sacred space. We loosen and open our bodies and our minds, consciously expanding and lifting our heart centre. We become aware of breathing in and breathing out, and rest back into ourselves in the present moment. We call in our intention to stay connected inside and with each other. We recognise that our song is our prayer and we hold our prayers in our hearts as we sing.

Practical Exercises

I have used these exercises with our choir to support the awareness of this type of sounding but they can also be done on your own. (They are easier to demonstrate than to describe in words.) The inspiration comes from Ruth Weimer, my voice teacher from the Lichtenberg Institute in Germany.

Allow plenty of time to work with these exercises, just doing a couple at a time.

Close your eyes. For a moment just be aware of breathing in and aware of breathing out...Relax down through the body, consciously softening the jaw, the shoulders, the belly etc. and listen as if your whole body was covered in ears. Listen to sounds far away, in the room... in your body. Try not to label them, just be present... big ears listening. Listen as if you are just a vast field of awareness not separate from what you are hearing. Are there inner pictures? Just notice what is here in this moment without trying to make anything happen. Are there sensations, places where you feel a pulse or a tingling inner aliveness? Become aware of your hands: can you sense inner aliveness (vibration) there? Now listen to the inner sounds in your head around the base of the skull... these cricket-like sounds... make friends with them. These are the same sounds that we can allow into our voice. You may want to learn them by heart.

Keeping your eyes closed listen to these sounds with your whole being. Allow yourself to be a resonance body: senses wide open, judging mind on pause. With a soft awareness, can you hear the high frequencies? Just notice. If you want, try closing off your ears and listening deeply to these inner sounds.

Sing "ahh". Begin just on one note – effortlessly, no push, casually, just receiving sound. Open to it. Allow it for a few minutes.

Suction: Now begin by feeling the bottoms of your feet; imagine that the soles of your feet are sucking up a leaf. Let that awareness be with you while you sing. Listen deeply with those full body ears.

Now imagine your ears are singing; they can have a sense of flying. The ear drums are being magnetised towards each other as you sing. Allow sounds all over your range. You can't do anything wrong if you listen deeply... start anywhere...

How much can you just receive the sound? Each tone innocent and new, like a child.

Remember you are 99% emptiness and that emptiness is singing.

Easy, effortless – receiving sound; it's a state.

> *What is the secret? According to the Sufis, it is the truth of our oneness or unity with the Divine. It is difficult to use words to describe this experience. ... [T]he bubble of the separate self dissolves and transforms into the Ocean. All definitions of ourselves—"I am this", "I am that"—are experienced as temporary illusions that veil us from the reality of our true Self.*

~ Joe Disabatino

RESOURCE 10: INQUIRIES WORTH PONDERING

I invite you to take your time with these inquiries, perhaps sharing them with a partner or friend and just reflecting on one or two a day.

- What or who have been the greatest teachers in your life?
- What is your deepest longing?
- What calls forth your greatest aliveness?
- What does fulfilment mean to you?
- What are you saying "Yes" (or "No") to in your life right now?
- What do you really love?
- What would be the next step that would carry you towards what you are really wanting?
- What is the life that wants to live you? What does your life want to be about?
- What magnifies your soul? Who/what are the people, activities or books that support that?
- What sufferings have seasoned you? What have you gleaned from these times?
- Is there anybody in your life that you need to forgive, but haven't? Can you make steps towards this?
- What do you value most in a friendship?
- Who or what inspires and enriches your life, and how?
- Who or what really challenges you?
- How do you know when it is time to let go of something or someone? What informs you?
- Do you listen to and act on your guidance?
- When do you feel most motivated, most inspired? How can you bring more of that into your life starting today?

- What could you make simpler, more focused in your daily life?
- What hurts you and causes you to suffer?
- What resentment, anguish or bitterness are you ready to let go of?
- What and who matters most to you? Is that reflected in how you use your time and energy?
- What supports you to be the best you can be? What gets in the way or drains your energy?
- What helps you open to inspiration? How could that be supported even more?
- What is grace? How does it appear in your life?
- How do you access/create sacred space in your life?
- Where were the major shifts and transitions in your life? The places of major growth? And why?
- What qualities do you want to call in to keep the magic in your life alive and well?
- What does it mean to be "free"? What would it take to be truly free?
- Is this body just your cloak, your vehicle or your real self?
- What makes life meaningful for you in this phase of your life?
- If you knew this was your last day, how would you choose to spend your day and with whom?

You can track what inspires you by asking these questions:

- Who or what inspired me today?
- Where did I experience a sense of peace and ease today?
- What made me happy today?

RESOURCE 11: INTENTIONS

Another tool for self-explorations is to examine your intentions. Ask yourself: at this point in my life, what are my intentions for the following? (This is quite a good resource for intentions at New Years: being clear about what you want to call in for yourself or how you might best want to support and encourage those you love.)

Myself-

My Partner / Love / Relationships-

Children-

Home-

Extended Family-

Friendships-

Spirituality/Growth-

Self Development-

Self Care-

Hobbies and Creativity-

Work/Service-

Community/World-

Learning-

Play-

Travel-

Other Explorations-

Where To From Here?

RESOURCE 12: EXPLORATIONS

Next time you are on retreat, or having a solitary self-exploration weekend or a sharing with your support group or partner, consider exploring some of the following as tools for self-discovery.

1. What makes my heart sing?
2. What do I value most, what is really important to me? What are my core values?
3. What do I *really* want from life?
4. What can I let go of now? What do I really want to keep?
5. How can I create more fun and laughter in my life?
6. What are my passions? What makes me feel alive?
7. In my journey so far, what have I not done which I would really like to do?
8. What have I lost along the way?
9. What kind of person do I want to be? Am I content with what is?
10. What understandings and insights are igniting me at the moment?
11. What would I include in a "great day"?
12. What do I really love about myself?
13. What is holding me back (if anything)? How can I overcome these obstacles?
14. What am I avoiding in this moment?
15. When is enough enough (in every area of my life)?
16. Is there anything I would like to transform in myself? How will I go about this? What is my first step?
17. How do I live my spirituality? How do I express it and where?
18. What would I like to leave behind when I am gone?
19. What and how do I contribute to making this planet a better place? A more enlightened planet?

20. Am I making a priority of being a conscious, awake being? How can I live with more presence?

21. Am I able to be in the moment, to let things go and just be here with what is?

22. Do I live from a place of gratitude and appreciation or do I get caught up in wanting things to be different than they are? (Check out gratefulness.org.)

23. What are my real gifts that I bring to life? Do I get a chance to really express and live them?

24. Do I live my life aware that all things are connected or do I tend to separate and judge?

25. Am I truly happy? At peace in myself? If not, what attitudes might I need to shift, and how?

26. When in my life did I stop singing? Dancing?

27. When did I stop being enchanted by stories? Comforted and nourished by silence?

28. What qualities do I want to bring to this phase of my life?

29. Who am I? What are the "stories" I tell myself? And when I go deeper, who am I really?

30. Finally, like Mary Oliver, can I ask myself, "What is it I plan to do with [my] one wild and precious life?" And just do it. Good luck!

With life as fleeting as a half-drawn breath,
we have no time to plant anything but love.

~adapted from Rumi[69]

At our core we are radiant beings of light with the capacity to uplift and bless all those we meet, offering loving kindness, compassion and joy. This awakened awareness, this state of being is our sacred gift back to life.

In gratitude for this extraordinary opportunity of our human existence. May we use it wisely.

From my heart, with love,
Blessings on your journey...

NOTES

[1] "Wind Beneath my Wings" was sung by Bette Midler.

[2] Unless I indicate otherwise, italicised translations are into Sanskrit, the language of ritual in Buddhism and Hinduism and a literary tradition in India, where it has often served as the common language between diverse cultures.

[3] Adyashanti at a discourse I attended at Mount Madonna in 2005.

[4] The origins of the familiar proverb "the journey is the goal" are unclear. In 1975, Theroux attributed it to Michael Frayn (1). More recently it is the title of an article by Bradford and Sterling, who find this concept is at the heart of Taoism and humanistic psychology (1).

[5] From the Bible, Philippians 4:7.

[6] See for example Pope and Singer (3, 102).

[7] Personal communication, Jun. 30, 2016. Estee – Helvi Lystiani – was our singing companion and yoga instructor in Ubud, Bali. See www.theyogabarn.com/bali-yoga-teachers.

[8] Unskilfulness has a specialised meaning in Buddist practice. The "ultimate goal of Buddhism" is to reduce suffering; skilful actions or thoughts promote that goal, while unskilful ones do not (Taniguchi 33). See "Buddhist Principles" – "the Four Noble Truths" for the causes and elimination of suffering.

[9] Rumi (109) asks us, "Don't you know. . . whatever you are seeking, you are its very essence?"; see also Meister Eckhart (31-32), "And what once you were seeking now seeks you . . ."

[10] See also Thich Nhat Hanh in *Teachings on Love* (143-144).

[11] A teaching story. This and many of my other "teaching stories" are familiar to many traditions. They are ancient parables from a variety of respected sources, passed down by teachers over the ages, and as such belong to no one individual but rather to all beings. I begin such parables with "*I have heard that once. . .*" and tell them in the form I orally use. Like this tale, most are Zen Buddhist or Sufi folklore, and the original authors and dates are disputed or unknown. Please assume that is the case unless otherwise indicated.

[12] Bhagwan Shree Rajneesh (1931-1990), at a discourse that I attended in 1977.

[13] Bhagwan Shree Rajneesh's discourse in 1977.

[14] On the obstacle of pride, see for example the last three lines of Kay Keys "21 Praises of Tara"; and Jesus' parable about the Pharisee and the publican or tax collector (Luke 18:9-14).

[15] See Hearn (*Daily Puja* 14).

[16] See Vivekananda.

[17] Atum O'Kane, personal communication, 07 Oct. 2016 in Bhutan.

[18] Definition of mindfulness is from oxforddictionaries.com.

[19] Meister Eckhart quoted in Goldstein and Stahl (75).

[20] Inspired by Br. David Steindl-Rast's "A Good Day"(54).

[21] Marchetti is quoting George Carlin in the title of her book.

[22]Buffy Sainte Marie recorded "God is Alive, Magic is Afoot" with lyrics by Leonard Cohen from *Beautiful Losers*; the derivation "the Goddess is alive, magic is afoot" is often attributed to Budapest (n.d.).

[23] This is an accepted Buddhist teaching, but the specific quotation is often attributed to Levine in *Gradual Awakening* (96).

[24] See for example Rinchen or O'Brien on "The Six Perfections" or buddhism.about.com/od/Paramitas/a/The-Six-Perfections.htm, accessed 11 Apr. 2016.

[25] See for example Krasno *et al.* (274).

[26] "Discourse on Mindful Breathing" quoted by Thich Nhat Hanh in *Living Buddha* (103).

[27] See for example Rinpoche and Schlim (100).

[28]Anonymous – a lovely saying, usually incorrectly attributed to Buddha (fakebuddhaquotes.com/when-you-realize-how-perfect-everything-is-you-will-tilt-your-head-back-and-laugh-at-the-sky/).

[29] Prema Dasara, founder of Tara Dhatu, cites traveling-light.net and taradhatu.net when using "The heart has the capacity to love everyone . . ." re her *Dance of the 21 Praises of Tara*. See for example www.meetup.com/GoddessStore/messages/9614922/accessed 30 Jul. 2016.

[30] Khan, *The Mysticism of Sound and Music* at "16. The Manifestation of Sound on the Physical Sphere" (76), accessed 17 Mar. 2016 at hazrat-inayat-khan.org/php/views.php?h1=10&h2=16.

[31] Khan, *The Mysticism of Sound and Music* at "4. The Mysticism of Sound", accessed 16 Mar. 2016 at hazrat-inayat-khan.org/php/views.php?h1=10&h2=4

[32] See for example Olsen 246-249.

[33] For more details, see the recent discussion in Harding.

[34] See the Lichtenberg Institute's website at www.voicelearningcentre.com/art.html, accessed 05 Sep. 2016.

[35] See for example Czlonka (160) and Sen (n.p.).

[36] Khan, *The Mysticism of Sound and Music* at "3. The Music of the Spheres", accessed 16 Mar. 2016 at hazrat-inayat-khan.org/php/views.php?h1=10&h2=3&h3=0.

[37] See Fred Shapiro on the origin of the "Serenity Prayer", probably first published by Reinhold Niebuhr in 1943 and "the most famous and beloved prayer of the 20th century".

[38] This accepted interpretation of the Buddha's teaching is sometimes attributed to Stephen Levine (*A Gradual Awakening*).

[39] Discourses; see for example www.dalailama.com/teachings/training-the-mind/verse-8 accessed 23 Aug. 2016.

[40] The last of Buddha's "Five Remembrances" as translated by Thich Nhat Hanh in *The Heart of the Buddha's Teaching* (122).

⁴¹ Lyubomirsky, updated by Lyubomirsky and Della Porta, and by Lyubomirsky and Layous.

⁴² Jack Kornfield (*After the Ecstasy* 103).

⁴³ Pema Chödrön (149).

⁴⁴ See Loomis; Siddharth Mungekar.

⁴⁵ See for example James Eldrid (81).

⁴⁶ "It is more blessed to give than to receive" (Bible, Acts 20:35).

⁴⁷ Perks (*I Wish You Enough*). Many have published the poem "I Wish You Enough" with variations of Perks' story. Bob Perks may have been first, in 2001, except his characters were a father and daughter.

⁴⁸ Other authors substitute a mother for the father, and end with the anonymous saying, "They say it takes a minute to find a special person. . ." See for example Josefina Hudson (114).

⁴⁹ Roger of Taizé 76.

⁵⁰ Adapted from the four questions in Katie and Mitchell (15) and on Byron Katie's website.

⁵¹ This version of the "Peace Prayer" and the story behind it (supposedly it was found on a holy card of St. Francis, written by an anonymous author in Normandy in 1915) was accessed 23 Aug. 2016 at franciscan-archive.org/patriarcha/peace.html.

⁵² *Powa (Phowa)* is a Buddhist meditation that many consider the most valuable and effective practice to offer around the time of death, often understood to transfer consciousness into the state of truth.

⁵³ See sleepfoundation.org/how-sleep-works/how-much-sleep-do-we-really-need, accessed 12 Mar. 2016.

⁵⁴ Penny Harvey (*Catch the Tide* 184, 185, 211, 234, 235).

⁵⁵Articles on dry skin brushing were accessed 11 Mar. 2016 at www.dermalinstitute.com/us/library/20_article_Methods_of_Exfoliation.html; and ahha.org/selfhelp-articles/support-the-lymphatic-system/.

⁵⁶ See Graf; Vormann and Remer; Schwalfenberg; and www.ncbi.nlm.nih.gov/pmc/articles/PMC3195546/ accessed 12 Mar. 2016.

⁵⁷ I.e. Smith and MacKinnon's *100 Mile Diet*.

⁵⁸ Archer.

⁵⁹ Rossato-Bennett, *"Alive Inside"*. See also www.aliveinside.us/#land accessed 16 Mar. 2016; and Powers citing Verghese.

⁶⁰ Duffy, "The Best Fitness Trackers for 2016". Accessed 12 Mar. 2016 at www.pcmag.com/article2/0,2817,2404445,00.asp.

⁶¹Fitbits® is a trademark registered to Fitbit, Inc. Accessed 12 Mar. 2016 at www.fitbit.com/ca/store?gclid=CLDc_NH5u8sCFYlrfgodNUMHow.

⁶² Nutriblaster ™ is a trademark by Capbran Holdings, LLC in Los Angeles, CA. See www.juicingdietworks.com/nutribullet/nutribullet-vs-juicer-what-you-ought-to-know-885, accessed 12 Mar. 2016.

[63] Hann, *Somatics*. See also www.somaticsed.com/whatIs.html accessed 12 Mar 2016.

[64] Download the app at www.headspace.com/ accessed 12 Mar. 2016.

[65] The importance of gratitude is emphasized throughout this book. See for example "Tools for the Journey" in Chapter 1, and "The Importance of Gratitude" in Chapter 7.

[66] Thich Nhat Hanh (*Being Peace* 15).

[67] See for example Burger (207-209).

[68] Rumi ("Moving Water" 79).

[69] Adapted from Rumi's "Every Tree" (85). Coleman Barks' translation reads, "With life as short as a half taken breath, don't plant anything but love".

WORKS CITED

Adyashanti. *Falling Into Grace: Insights on the End of Suffering.* Sounds True, 2011.

Adyashanti. "5-Night Retreat." Open Gate Sangha, Mount Madonna Center, Watsonville, CA, 3-8 May 2005. Satsang Discourse.

Adyashanti. "5-Night Retreat." Open Gate Sangha, Asilomar Conference Centre, Pacific Grove, CA, 25 Feb to 02 Mar 2007. Discourse.

Amodeo, John. "The One Way – a New Spirit of Ecumenicalism." *Yoga Journal,* issue 23, Nov-Dec 1978.

Archer, Dale. "Violence, the Media and Your Brain." *Psychologytoday.com,* 02 Sep. 2013, www.psychologytoday.com/blog/reading-between-the-headlines/201309/violence-the-media-and-your-brain. Accessed 12 Mar 2016.

Arrien, Angeles. *The Second Half of Life: Opening the Eight Gates of Wisdom.* Sounds True, 2006.

Bailey, Alice. *Esoteric Psychology: A Treatise on the Seven Rays* (Vol. 1). Lucis Publishing, 1936.

Blake, William. *The Marriage of Heaven and Hell.* 1790. Oxford UP, 1975.

Bolen, Jean S. *Goddesses in Every Woman: Powerful Archetypes in Women's Lives.* 1984. HarperCollins, 2004.

Braden, Gregg. *Awakening to Zero Point: The Collective Initiation.* Radio Bookstore Press, 1993.

Bradford, G. Kenneth, and Molly M. Sterling. "The Journey Is the Goal: The Legacy of James F. T. Bugental." *Journal of Humanistic Psychology,* vol. 49, no. 3, 2009, pp. 316–328.

Brown, Mark. *Live Like a Window Work Like a Mirror: Enlightenment and the Practice of Eternity Consciousness.* First Light Books, 2011.

Budapest, Zsuzsanna. "The Goddess Is Alive and Magic Is Afoot." In Tess Whitehurst. "Hollywood's Superstars of the Soul." *Whole Life Times,* n.d., www.wholelifetimes.com/833/l-a-%E2%80%99s-superstars-of-the-soul/. Accessed 12 Feb. 2016.

Buddha. "Discourse on Mindful Breathing." In Thich Nhat Hanh. *Living Buddha, Living Christ.* 1997. Riverhead Books, 2007.

Buddha. "The Wise Man." *Dhammapada: The Sayings of the Buddha.* Translated by Thomas Byrom. 1976. Shambhala, 1993.

Burger, Bruce. *Esoteric Anatomy: The Body as Consciousness.* 1998. North Atlantic Books, 2012.

Byrom, Thomas, translator. *The Heart of Awareness: A Translation of the Ashtavakra Gita.* Shambhala, 1990.

Campbell, Joseph. *Pathways to Bliss: Mythology and Personal Transformation.* Edited by David Kudler. New World Library, 2004.

Capra, Fritjof. *The Tao of Physics: An Exploration of the Parallels Between Modern Physics and Eastern Mysticism.* 5th ed. Shambhala, 2010.

Carver, Raymond. "Late Fragment." In Aislinn Hunter. "How Poems Work: Late Fragment by Raymond Carver." *Globe and Mail,* 21 Dec. 2002, www.theglobeandmail.com/arts/how-poems-work/article1029144/. Accessed 05 Feb. 2016.

Chödrön, Pema. *Comfortable with Uncertainty: 108 Teachings on Cultivating Fearlessness and Compassion.* Shambhala, 2003.

Chodron, Thubten, and His Holiness the Dalai Lama (Foreward). *Open Heart, Clear Mind.* Snow Lion Publications, 1990.

Cockburn, Bruce. *Joy Will Find a Way.* True North Records, 1975.

Cohen, Leonard. "God is Alive, Magic is Afoot." *Beautiful Losers.* Viking Press, 1966.

Conroy, Susan. *Mother Teresa's Lessons of Love and Secrets of Sanctity.* Our Sunday Visitor Publishing, 2003.

Coward, Harold. *Perfectibility of Human Nature in Eastern and Western Thought.* State University of New York Press, 2008.

Czlonka, Rod. *Decide to Live.* Czlonka Media Group, 2007.

Chodron, Pema. *Start Where You Are: A Guide to Compassionate Living.* Shambhala, 2001.

Dasara, Prema. "The Heart Has the Capacity to Love Everyone." *Tara Dhatu,* n.d. , www.taradhatu.net/about/what-is-tara-dhatu/. Accessed 30 Jul 2016.

Dass, Ram, and Stephen Levine. *Grist for the Mill: Awakening to Oneness.* HarperCollins, 2014.

Deschene, Lorrie. "33 Things to Accept and Embrace." *Tiny Buddha,* 2012, tinybuddha.com/blog/33-things-to-accept-and-embrace/. Accessed 22 Nov. 2015.

Diaz, Cameron. *The Body Book: The Law of Hunger, the Science of Strength, and Other Ways to Love Your Amazing Body.* Harper Wave, 2014, pp. 87-89.

Disabatino, Joe. "A Sufi's Perspective on Relationships." *Yogi Times,* 2014, www.yogitimes.com/article/sufism-relationships-four-layers-of-heart. Accessed 28 Jan. 2016.

Dowrick, Stephanie. *Guided Meditations: Grace and Courage.* Bolinda, 2001. CD.

Dowrick, Stephanie. *Heaven on Earth: Timeless Prayers of Wisdom and Love.* Penguin, 2013.

Dowrick, Stephanie. *The Universal Heart: A Practical Guide to Love.* 2000. Allen & Unwin, 2012.

Eckhart, Meister. *Everything as Divine: The Wisdom of Meister Eckhart (Spiritual Samplers).* Translated by Edmund Colledge, and Bernard McGinn. Paulist Press, 1996.

Einstein, Albert. *Out of My Later Years: The Scientist, Philosopher and Man Portrayed Through His Own Words.* Philosophical Library, 1956, p. 13.

Eldrid, James A. *A Depth of Insight: One Man's Discipleship with Christ.* WestBow Press, 2013.

Ernst, Lisa. "Daylong Mindfulness Meditation Retreat." *The Lotus Blooms in the Mud.* 29 Jan. 2013, thelotusbloomsinthemud.com/2013/01/. Accessed 10 Jan. 2015.

Gibran, Kahlil. *The Prophet.* 1923. Wordsworth Classics, 1997.

Goldsmith, Joel S. *Conscious Union with God: Understanding the Truth.* 1962. Start Publishing, 2012. [Kobo version].

Goldsmith, Joel S. *The Infinite Way.* 1947. Willing, 1956.

Goldsmith, Joel. *The Realisation of Oneness.* Edited by Lorraine Sinkler. Allen & Unwin, 1968.

Goldstein, Elisha, and Bob Stahl. *MBSR Every Day: Daily Practice from the Heart of Mindfulness-Based Stress Reduction.* New Harbinger Publications, 2015.

Gray, John. *Men Are from Mars, Women Are from Venus.* HarperCollins, 1992.

Graf, Jeannette. *Stop Aging, Start Living: The Revolutionary 2-Week pH Diet.* Crown, 2007.

Gyatso, Tenzin, the 14th Dalai Lama. "Compassion and the Individual." *Dalailama.com,* n.d., www.dalailama.com/messages/compassion. Accessed 06 Mar. 2016.

Hafiz. *The Gift.* Translated by Daniel Ladinsky. Penguin, 1999.

Hafiz. "How Does It Feel to Be a Heart." *I Heard God Laughing: Poems of Hope and Joy: Renderings of Hafiz.* Translated by Daniel Ladinsky. 1996. Penguin, 2006.

Hanh, Thich Nhat. "Awakening the Heart: The Practice of Inner Transformation." *MindfulnessExercises.com,* 11 Oct. 2013. DVD.

Hanh, Thich Nhat, represented by Thich Chan Phap An. "Beginning Anew." *Buddhism Responding to the Needs of the 21st Century. Appendix 7: How to Enjoy Your Stay in Plum Village.* The World Buddhist Forum, Hangzhou, China, 13-16 Apr. 2006, Conference Presentation, pvfhk.org/index.php/en/studies-practices/29-transcripts/dt-. Accessed 10 May 2016.

Hanh, Thich Nhat. *Being Peace.* 1987. Parallax Press, 2005.

Hanh, Thich Nhat. "Freedom is not Given to Us." *Awakening the Heart* Mindfulness Retreat, University of British Columbia, Vancouver, BC, Canada. 8-13 Aug 2011. Discourse.

Hanh, Thich Nhat. *The Heart of the Buddha's Teaching.* 1997. Harmony, 1999.

Hanh, Thich Nhat. *Living Buddha, Living Christ.* 1997. Riverhead Books, 2007.

Hanh, Thich Nhat. *The Long Road Turns to Joy: A Guide to Walking Meditation by Thich Nhat Hanh.* 2004. Parallax Press, 2011, p. 46.

Hanh, Thich Nhat. "Loosening the Knots of Anger Through Mindfulness Practice." *Lion's Roar.* LionsRoar.com, 2001, www.lionsroar.com/loosening-the-knots-of-anger/. Accessed 30 Jan. 2016.

Hanh, Thich Nhat. *Teachings on Love.* 2007. Parallax Press, 2013.

Hanh, Thich Nhat. "Waking Up." *Work: How to find Joy and Meaning in Each Hour of the Day.* Parallax Press, 2008.

Hanna, Thomas. *Somatics: Reawakening the Mind's Control of Movement, Flexibility, and Health*. 1998. Da Capo Press, 2004.

Harding, C. Lance. *Mysteries of the Vitruvian Man*. Academy Of Sacred Geometry, 9 Apr. 2014, academysacredgeometry.com/courses/mysteries-vitruvian-man. Accessed 05 Sep. 2016.

Harvey, Penny. *Catch the Tide: Plan Now for Your Ultimate Retirement*, 2013.

Hearn, Tarchin. "Bodhisattva Vow." *Daily Puja: Contemplations to Orient the Mind Towards Awakening*. 1993. Wangapeka Books, 2007, greendharmatreasury.org/wp-content/uploads/2013/10/DP-5th-Ed-hi-res.pdf. Accessed 9 Mar. 2016.

Hearn, Tarchin. "Deep Healing." *Green Dharma Treasury*. 2010, greendharmatreasury.org/practices/deep-healing. Accessed 09 Mar. 2016.

Hearn, Tarchin. "Frequently I Pause." *Daily Puja: Contemplations to Orient the Mind Towards Awakening*. Wangapeka Books, 2007, greendharmatreasury.org/wp-content/uploads/2013/10/DP-5th-Ed-hi-res.pdf. Accessed 9 Mar. 2016.

Hearn, Tarchin. "Recipe for Misery." *Coming to Your Senses (Karunakarma Series: Vol. 2)*. Wangapeka Books, 2002, pp. 10.-11, www.wangapeka.org/wp-content/uploads/2012/09/EbookComingToYourSenses.pdf . Accessed Feb. 2016.

Hearn, Tarchin. "Taking Refuge." *Daily Puja: Contemplations to Orient the Mind Towards Awakening*. Wangapeka Books, 2007, greendharmatreasury.org/wp-content/uploads/2013/10/DP-5th-Ed-hi-res.pdf. Accessed 09 Mar. 2016.

Houston, Jean. *A Passion for the Possible: A Guide to Realizing Your True Potential*. HarperCollins, 1998.

Hudson, Josefina U. *Beautiful Words of Life: From the Internet with Love*. Xlibris Corp, 2008.

Jeffers, Susan. *Feel the Fear… and Do It Anyway*. 1987. Random House, 2006.

Kabir. "All Know That the Ocean Merges Into the Drop." In John Baldock. *The Essence of Sufism*. Chartwell Books, 2005.

Kabir. "Friend, Hope for the Guest." *Kabir: Ecstatic Poems*. Edited and translated by Robert Bly. 1977. Beacon Press, 2004.

Kapleau, Philip, editor. *The Wheel of Death: Writings from Zen Buddhist and Other Sources*. 1972. Routledge, 2008.

Katie, Byron. "The Work of Byron Katie: An Introduction." *TheWork.com*, 2015, thework.com/sites/thework/downloads/little_book/English_LB.pdf. Accessed 28 Jan. 2016.

Katie, Byron, and Stephen Mitchell. *Loving What Is: Four Questions That Can Change Your Life*. Harmony Books, 2002.

Keys, Kay. "Twenty One Praises of Tara." *Kay's Spirit Page*, 2005, kaykeys.net/spirit/buddhism/taradance/tara21.html. Accessed 30 Jul.

2016.

Khan, Hazrat Inayat. *The Inner Life (Volume 1 of the Sufi Message of Hazrat Inayat Khan)*. Hunter House, 1974.

Khan, Hazrat Inayat. *The Music of Life*. Omega, 1983.

Khan, Hazrat Inayat. "The Mysticism of Sound and Music." *The Sufi Message of Hazrat Inayat Khan* (Vol. 2). 1960. Shambhala, 1996, at Chapter III.

Khan, Hazrat Inayat. *The Sayings of Hazrat Inayat Khan*. 1975. Library of Alexandria, 2003.

Khan, Hazrat Inayat. *Unity of Religious Ideals (Volume 9 of the Sufi Message of Hazrat Inayat Khan)*. 1979. Motilal Banarsidass, 1990.

Knight, Goldie. *Journey of the Soul*. iUniverse, 2000.

Kornfield, Jack. *After the Ecstasy the Laundry: How the Heart Grows Wise on the Spiritual Path*. Bantam Books, 2001.

Kornfield, Jack. *Living Buddhist Masters*. Prajñā Press, 1977.

Krasno, Jeff, Sarah Herrington, and Nicole Lindstrom. *Wanderlust: A Modern Yogi's Guide to Discovering Your Best Self*. Rodale, 2015.

Lai, Whalen. "Ch'an Metaphors: Waves, Water, Mirror, Lamp." *Philosophy East & West*, vol. 29, no. 3, July 1979, pp. 245-253, www.thezensite.com/ZenEssays/HistoricalZen/ChanMetaphors.htm. Accessed 04 Jan. 2016.

Lambdin, Thomas O., translator. "Verse 22." *The Gospel of Thomas*. Gnostic Society Library, The Nag Hammadi Library, n.d., www.gnosis.org/naghamm/gthlamb.html. Accessed 13 Nov. 2015.

Lao-Tzu. "Empty Yourself of Everything." *Tao Te Ching*. Translated by Gia-Fu Feng and Jane English. 1972. Vintage Books, 1997, c. 16.

Lao-Tzu. "The Highest Good is Like Water." *Tao Te Ching*. Translated by Gia-Fu Feng and Jane English. Vintage Books, 1997, c. 8.

Levine, Stephen. *A Gradual Awakening*. 1979. Anchor Books, 1989.

Levine, Stephen. *Guided Meditations, Explorations and Healings*. Anchor Books, 1991.

Lisieux, St. Therese. "Peace Within." In "Spirituality and You." *JenningsCentre.org*, 2015, jenningscenter.org/news/peace-within. Accessed 08 Feb. 2016.

Lichtenberg Institute. "The Art of Listening." Voice Learning Centre, n.d., www.voicelearningcentre.com/art.html. Accessed 05 Sep. 2016.

Logan, Jeremy. "The Heart of Understanding". Wangapeka Study & Retreat Centre, 2016, www.wangapeka.org/programme/the-heart-of-understanding/. Accessed 28 Jul. 2016.

Loomis, Carol J. "The $600 Billion Challenge." *Times Inc. Fortune*, 16 Jun. 2010, fortune.com/2010/06/16/the-600-billion-challenge/. Accessed 06 Jan. 2016.

Loy, David R. *A New Buddhist Path: Enlightenment, Evolution and Ethics in the Modern World*. Wisdom Publications, 2015.

Lyubomirsky, Sonja. "The Science of Interventions for Increasing Well-Being." *The Science of Well-Being and Implications for Societal Quality of Life*. AAAS

2010 Annual Meeting, San Diego, CA, 20 Feb. 2010. Conference Presentation.

Lyubomirsky, Sonja, and Kristin Layous. "How Do Simple Positive Activities Increase Well-Being?" *Current Directions in Psychological Science*, vol. 22, no. 1, pp. 57-62.

Lyubomirsky, Sonja, and Matthew D. Della Porta. "Boosting Happiness, Buttressing Resilience: Results from Cognitive and Behavioral Interventions." *Handbook of Adult Resilience*. Edited by John W. Reich, Alex J. Zautra, and John S. Hall. Guilford Press, 2010, pp. 450-464.

Mana Retreat Centre, 2015, manaretreat.com. Accessed 08 Feb. 2016.

Marchetti, Sandra. *Men Are from Earth, Women Are from Earth... Deal with It.* Coal Under Pressure Publications, 2013.

Merton, Thomas. *Conjectures of a Guilty Bystander*. Doubleday Religion, 1968.

Midler, Bette. "Wind Beneath My Wings." *Beaches*. Rhino Atlantic, 2012.

Moore, Robert L. *The Archetype of Initiation*. Edited by Max J. Havlick. Xlibris, 2001.

Moore, Robert, and Douglas Gillette. *King, Warrior, Magician, Lover: Rediscovering the Archetypes of the Mature Masculine*. HarperCollins, 1991.

Moore, Thomas. *Care of the Soul: A Guide for Cultivating Depth and Sacredness in Everyday Life*. HarperCollins, 1992.

Morgan, Diane. *Essential Buddhism: A Comprehensive Guide to Belief and Practice*. ABC-CLIO, 2010.

Munindo, Ajahn. *The Gift of Well-Being: Joy, Sorrow and Renunciation on the Buddha's Way. Six Talks by Ajahn Munindo*. River Publications, 1997. Free download, www.saraniya.com/page/ebooks/ajahn-munindo-the-gift-of-well-being.html. Accessed 01 Dec. 2015

Mungekar, Siddharth. "Bill Gates . . ." *Quora*, 17 Jun. 2014, www.quora.com/Bill-Gates-donated-about-28-billion-when-he-was-worth-50-billion-Now-he-is-worth-80-billion-How-does-his-net-worth-keep-going-up-when-he-had-parted-with-half-of-his-fortune. Accessed 06 Jun 2016.

O'Brien, Barbara. "Samsara." *About Religion*, 04 Sep. 2015, buddhism.about.com/od/abuddhistglossary/g/Samsaradef.htm. Accessed 07 Nov. 2015.

O'Brien, Barbara. "The Six Perfections." *About Religion*, 04 Nov. 2015, buddhism.about.com/od/Paramitas/a/The-Six-Perfections.htm. Accessed 13 Feb. 2016.

Oliver, Mary. "The Summer Day." *New and Selected Poems, Volume 1*. 1992. Beacon Press, 2004, p. 94.

Olsen, Brad. *Modern Esoteric: Beyond Our Senses*. Consortium of Collective Consciousness, 2014.

Oman, Maggie. *Prayers for Healing*. Coneri Press, 1997.

Palmer, Harry. "Exercise 17: Compassion." *Resurfacing®: Techniques for Exploring Consciousness*. Star's Edge Creations, 1997.

Palmo, Ani Tenzin. *Reflections on a Mountain Lake: Teachings on Practical Buddhism.* Snow Lion Publications, 2002.

Pay it Forward. Directed by Mimi Leder. Warner Bros., 2000.

Perks, Bob. *I Wish You Enough: Embracing Life's Most Valuable Moments… One Wish at a Time.* 2001. Thomas Nelson, 2009.

Pilgrim, Peace. *Peace Pilgrim: Her Life and Work in Her Own Words.* 1983. Ocean Tree Books, 1992.

Pope, Kenneth S., and Jerome L. Singer, editors. *The Stream of Consciousness: Scientific Investigations Into the Flow of Human Experience (Emotions, Personality and Psychotherapy).* 1978. Plenum Press, 2012.

Powers, Richard. "Use It or Lose It: Dancing Makes You Smarter." *Standford Dance,* 2010, socialdance.stanford.edu/syllabi/smarter.htm. Accessed 16 Mar. 2016.

Rilke, Rainer Maria. *Letters to a Young Poet.* Translated by Mark Harman. 1903. Cambridge UP, 2011.

Rinchen, Geshe S., translator and Ruth S. Sonam, editor. *The Six Perfections.* Snow Lion, 1998. [Kindle Version].

Rinpoche, Chokyi N. and David R. Shlim. *Medicine and Compassion: A Tibetan Lama's Guidance for Caregivers.* Wisdom Publications, 2006.

Roger of Taizé. *God Is Love Alone.* GIA Publications, 2003.

Roman, Sanaya. *Personal Power Through Awareness: A Guidebook for Sensitive People.* H J Kramer, 1986.

Rossato-Bennett, Michael, producer and director. *Alive Inside.* Video Service Corp., 2014.

Roshi, Shunryu S. *Zen Mind, Beginner's Mind: 40th Anniversary Edition.* 1970. Shambhala, 2010.

Rumi, Jalāl. "On the Day I Die." *The Soul of Rumi: A New Collection of Ecstatic Poems.* Translated by Coleman Barks. HarperCollins, 2002.

Rumi, Jalāl. "At the End of My Life." *The Soul of Rumi: A New Collection of Ecstatic Poems.* Translated by Coleman Barks. HarperCollins, 2002.

Rumi, Jalāl. "Every tree." *The Glance: Songs of Soul-Meeting.* Translated by Coleman Barks. Penguin, 2001.

Rumi, Jalāl. "Grief Can Be the Garden of Compassion." *Bringing Your Soul to Light: Healing Through Past Lives and the Time Between.* Edited by Linda Backman. Llewellyn Publications, 2009.

Rumi, Jalāl. "Keep Walking…Don't Move the Way Fear Makes You Move." *Unseen Rain: Quatrains of Rumi.* Translated by John Moyne, and Coleman Barks. 1986. Shambhala, 2001.

Rumi, Jalāl. "Let the Beauty." *The Essential Rumi: New Expanded Edition.* Translated by Coleman Barks, with Reynold Nicholson, A.J. Arberry, and John Moyne. 1995. HarperCollins, 2004, p. 36.

Rumi, Jalāl. *Like This: 43 Odes.* Translated by Coleman Barks. Maypap, 1990.

Rumi, Jalāl. *Love's Ripening: Rumi on the Heart's Journey.* Translated by Kabir Helminski, and Ahmad Rezwani. 2008. Shambhala, 2010.

Rumi, Jalāl. "Moving Water." *The Soul of Rumi: A New Collection of Ecstatic Poems.* Translated by Coleman Barks. HarperCollins, 2002.

Rumi, Jalāl. "O Love." In Sogyal Rinpoche. *The Tibetan Book of Living and Dying.* Edited by Patrick Gaffney, and Andrew Harvey. 1992. HarperCollins, 2012.

Rumi, Jalāl. "Out Beyond Our Ideas." In Frederick Quinn. *Welcoming the Interfaith Future: Religious Pluralism in a Global Age.* Peter Lang Publishing, 2012.

Rumi, Jalāl. "That Lives in Us." *Love Poems from God: Twelve Sacred Voices from the East and West.* Translated by Daniel Ladinsky. Penguin, 2002.

Rumi, Jalāl. "Trust in God, but First Tether Your Camel." In John Baldock. *The Essence of Rumi.* Chartwell Books, 2005, p. 148.

Rumi, Jalāl. "Be the Soul of That Place." *One Song: A New Illuminated Rumi.* Illustrated by Michael Green. Running Press, 2005.

Sainte Marie, Buffy. "God Is Alive, Magic Is Afoot." *Illuminations.* Vanguard, 1969.

Santosh. "The Mani Man." *Stories of Kindness from Around the World.* Kindspring.org. 09 Dec. 2007, www.kindspring.org/story/view.php?sid=8004. Accessed 02 Jan. 2016.

Schwalfenberg, Gerry K. "The Alkaline Diet: Is There Evidence That an Alkaline Ph Diet Benefits Health?" *J Environ Public Health,* 2012: 727630.

Sen, Paul. "Tiny Finding That Opened New Frontier." *BBC News,* 25 Jul. 2007, news.bbc.co.uk/2/hi/science/nature/6914175.stm ; *Jefferson Lab,* education.jlab.org/qa/how-much-of-an-atom-is-empty-space.htm. Accessed 05 Feb. 2016.

Seng-Ts'an, Third Zen Patriarch. *The Hsin Hsin Ming, Verses on the Faith-Mind.* Translated by Richard Clarke. 1973. White Pine Press, 2001.

Shapiro, Fred. "I Was Wrong About the Serenity Prayer." *Huffingpost,* 15 May 2014, www.huffingtonpost.com/2014/05/15/serenity-prayer-origin_n_5331924.html. Accessed 10 Feb. 2016.

Shyam, Swami. *Light of Knowledge.* 1962. 1976.

Singh, Taran, editor. *Teachings of Guru Nanak Dev. Pattala.* Punjabi University, 2001.

Smith, Alisa, and J.B. MacKinnon. *The 100-Mile Diet: A Year of Local Eating.* Random House, 2007.

Steindl-Rast, David. *David Steindl-Rast: Essential Writings.* Orbis Books, 2010.

Steindl-Rast, David, Louie Schwartzberg, and Patricia Carlson. *A Good Day: A Gift of Gratitude.* Sterling Ethos, 2013.

Stephens, Michael. *Provolution: A Guide to Changing the World Through Personal Evolution.* John Hunts Publishing, 2010.

Stone, Merlin. *When God Was a Woman.* Harcourt Brace, 1976.

Strayed, Cheryl. *Brave Enough.* Knopf, 2015.

Tagore, Rabindranath. "Love is the Only Reality." In Gordon M. Burnham.

Meditation Tips 'n Techniques. Spirit Flame Publishing, 2013.

Tagore, Rabindranath. "A New Day." *1,001 Pearls of Wisdom.* Edited by David Ross. Chronicle Books, 2006.

Taniguchi, Shoyo. "Methodology of Buddhist Biomedical Ethics." *Religious Ethics and Resources in Bioethics.* Edited by Paul F. Camenisch. Springer-Science + Business Media, 1994.

Theroux, Paul. *The Great Railway Bazaar.* Houghton Mifflin, 1975.

Tolle, Eckhart. *Living the Liberated Life and Dealing with the Pain Body (Teaching Series).* Sounds True, 2001. CD.

Tolle, Eckhart. *A New Earth: Awakening to Your Life's Purpose.* 2005. Penguin, 2008.

Tolle, Eckhart. *The Power of Now: A Guide to Spiritual Enlightenment.* 1999. New World Library, and Namaste Publishing, 2010.

Tolle, Eckhart. *Practicing the Power of Now.* New World Library, 1999.

Tolle, Eckhart. *Realisation of Being (Power of Now Teaching Series).* Sounds True, 2001. CD.

Tolle, Eckhart. *Stillness Speaks.* New World Library, and Namaste Publishing, 2003.

Verghese, Joe, *et al.* "Leisure Activities and the Risk of Dementia in the Elderly." *N Engl J Med,* 2003, vol. 348, pp. 2508-2516.

Vivekananda. "Jnana-Yoga." *The Complete Works of Swami Vivekananda* (Vol. 2). Advaita Ashrama, 1900, c. 12.

Vormann, Juergen, and Tomas Remer. "Dietary, Metabolic, Physiologic, and Disease-Related Aspects of Acid-Base Balance: Foreword to the Contributions of the Second International Acid-Base Symposium." *J. Nutr.,* vol. 138, no. 2, 2008, pp. 413S-414S.

Weeks, Bradford S. "The Physician, the Ear, and Sacred Music." *Music: Physician for Times to Come.* Edited by Don Campbell. Quest Books Theosophical Publishing House, 1991.

Whitman, Walt. "Song of Myself." *Leaves of Grass: The Original 1855 Edition.* Dover Publications, 2007.

Williamson, Marianne. *A Return to Love: Reflections on the Principles of a Course in Miracles.* HarperCollins, 1992, marianne.com/. Accessed 05 Feb. 2016.

Yogananda, Paramahansa. *Scientific Healing Affirmations.* 1924. Self Realization Fellowship, 1998.

Zubko, Andy. *Treasury of Spiritual Wisdom.* Blue Dove Press, 1996.

PERMISSIONS

The author is very grateful to the following for permission to use the fine materials from their books, websites and/or discourses in this work.

Adyashanti generously granted permission to quote the excerpt from his book *Falling Into Grace*, and material from my notes and memories of his discourses at Open Gate Sangha's retreats in California in 2005 and 2007.

Many thanks to Beacon Press for permission to use Robert Bly's version of Kabir's poem beginning "Friend, hope for the guest" from *Kabir: Ecstatic Poems*.

Stephanie Dowrick's poem beginning "There is no other way to love but generously" is from *Heaven on Earth* (published by Penguin), adapted from *The Universal Heart* (published by Allen & Unwin), and is reproduced with the kind permission of the author.

My profound gratitude goes to Thich Nhat Hanh and Unified Buddhist Church Publishing for permission to use material from the notes I took at Thây's discourses and other quotations from his teachings, as well as "Beginning Anew" (in Resource 7) from the Plum Village orientation booklet *How to Enjoy Your Stay in Plum Village*.

Tarchin Hearn's *bodhisattva* vow and poem beginning "Frequently I pause" from his eBook *Daily Puja*, and an excerpt from his contemplation on "gifts from the green plants" from *Deep Healing*, are reprinted with the author's kind permission. All three are available on his *Green Dharma Treasury* website at greendharmatreasury.org. The "Recipe for Misery" from Tarchin Hearn's eBook *Coming to Your Senses* is summarised by permission of the author.

I would like to thank Daniel Ladinsky and Penguin Publications for allowing me to use the following two poems:

> Rumi, "That Lives in Us," translated by Daniel Ladinsky, from *Love Poems from God: Twelve Sacred Voices from the East and West* (New York: Penguin, 2002). Copyright © 2002 by Daniel Ladinsky and used with his permission; and

> Hafiz, an excerpt from "How Does it Feel to be a Heart", translated

by Daniel Ladinsky, from the Penguin publication *I Heard God Laughing: Poems of Hope and Joy.* Copyright © 1999 Daniel Ladinsky and used with his permission.

The "Compassion Exercise", one of 30 exercises that can be found in *Resurfacing®: Techniques for Exploring Consciousness* by Harry Palmer, is reprinted with the permission of the author. ReSurfacing® is a registered trademark of Star's Edge, Inc.

Deep thanks to Swami Shyam for permission to use his inspired teachings throughout the book. These come from my notes and memory. I backed them up where possible by citations from Swami-Ji's written work.

Grateful thanks to Namaste Publishing of PO Box 62084, Vancouver, BC, Canada for permission to use the quotations in this work from Eckhart Tolle's inspirational books *The Power of Now: A Guide to Spiritual Enlightenment* (2010), copyright © 1999 Eckhart Tolle and *Stillness Speaks* (2010), copyright © 2003 Eckhart Tolle.

The following illustrations are used by permission of the named copyright holders:

Cover, © Rainer Huebner, *Isis Temple*, text added, 1997, personal photograph.

Figure 1. Mana Retreat Centre from the garden, © Mana Charitable Trust, *Mana*, text added, manaretreat.com, 2009, 16 Mar. 2016.

Figure 2. View from the sanctuary at Mana Retreat Centre, © Mana Charitable Trust, *Mana Sanctuary*, text added, manaretreat.com, 2009, 02 Dec. 2015.

Chapter 2 opener, © Sasha Huebner, *The Still Point*, 2014, personal photograph.

Chapter 3 opener, © Rainer Huebner, *Shanti and Rainer*, Jul. 2014, personal photograph.

Figure 3. Goddess of compassion, Kwan Yin (Tara), welcomes all to the Sanctuary at Mana Retreat Centre, © Mana Charitable Trust, *Goddess Tara*, text added, manaretreat.com, 2009, 02 Dec. 2015.

Figure 4. The Goddess Way forest trail, Mana Retreat Centre, © Mana Charitable Trust, *Goddess Way*, text added, manaretreat.com, 2009, 02 Dec. 2015.

Figure 5. Fibonacci / golden spiral, adapted by the author from Dicklyon, Wikimedia Commons, public domain, *Fibonacci Spiral 34*, commons.wikimedia.org/wiki/File:Fibonacci_spiral_34.svg, 17 Mar 2008,

10 Sep. 2016. Concept by the mathematician Leonardo Pisano a.k.a. Fibonacci (c. 1170-1250).

Figure 6. Leonardo da Vinci's drawing, from Leonardo da Vinci, *Canon of Proportions*, 1490. Public domain.

Figure 7. Author with her four children, © Rainer Huebner, *Tanya's Wedding Day*, text added, 10 Mar. 2012, personal photograph.

Resource 5 opener, © Nyssa Hutton, *View from Mana*, 2014, personal photograph.

"About the Author" opener, © Jade Ferriere, *Shanti*, Dec. 2015, personal photograph.

Spirit of love, be with us today.
Guide us. Ignite us with the fire
Of your presence and your love.

ABOUT THE AUTHOR

Shanti lives with her beloved partner Rainer in the bush-clad hills of the Coromandel (New Zealand), overlooking the ocean. She is a mother of four beautiful beings and has six delightful grandchildren. She is one of the three founders of Mana Retreat Centre as well as one of the trustees/guardians of this exquisite Centre for "the exploration and awakening of consciousness" (which has been a big part of her life's work). She is a certified Hakomi therapist, a mentor for the Dances of Universal Peace and a marriage celebrant. Originally she trained as a social worker, but her journey took her in many diverse directions. Some of her great joys are yoga and meditation (a 40 year veteran of both), singing with her choir, dancing, walking in nature, massage, health and well-being, tending her grandchildren and her garden, and travelling to and studying at centres around the globe as well as visiting sacred sites and inspirational teachers.

Shanti celebrates and acknowledges that there are many paths to the Light. Her root teacher was Swami Shyam; in her 20's she lived in the mountains of India as one of his students, and she returns at intervals for renewal. She has a special affinity for the goddesses of antiquity and the Sufi tradition. She has attended a Christian Bible College, and most years spends a week singing at the Taizé Christian monastery. She has studied the Tao, Hinduism and done a Ph.D. in metaphysics. Many of her practices have their roots in Zen Buddhism. Honouring all paths to the One, she encourages us to let our light shine, to be our own unique self, to celebrate and give thanks for this precious gift of life, to awaken to our true nature, and to offer our gifts to the world. She invites us to share what she has gleaned and as we read, to accompany her for a few hours on this journey of "Finding the Luminous Field".

Made in the USA
San Bernardino, CA
12 December 2016